"In Abby Seiff's rendition, the Tonle nymphlike, alluring and magical, like the walls of Cambodian temples at the at other times, meshed into the lives of of it. Seiff's *Troubling the Water* is a beat .... powerful ode to an ancient but rapidly disappearing world of interdependence between people and nature. A gifted writer and sensitive observer, she re-creates a world readers will want to save. A must-read."

—SAUMYA ROY, author of *Castaway Mountain: Love and Loss among the Wastepickers of Mumbai*

"Abby Seiff has courageously covered Cambodia's troubling trajectory in the twenty-first century. This book is her testament to the life and death of the largest freshwater lake in Southeast Asia, one of the most productive inland fisheries in the world, a people and way of life quickly disappearing."

—SOPHAL EAR, author of *Aid Dependence in Cambodia: How Foreign Assistance Undermines Democracy*

"A powerful book that perfectly captures the vulnerabilities of one of the world's most important lakes, Cambodia's Tonle Sap, by documenting the fragility of life for the millions who subsist on its floodplain. Seiff's painstaking research, coupled with her years of reporting from Cambodia, gives voice to the marginalized and the unheard. *Troubling the Water* is a unique, lyrical, and immensely readable account of the impact posed by the building of dams on the Mekong and of the profound risks that the lake's demise holds for a nation. Highly recommended."

—ROBERT CARMICHAEL, author of *When the Clouds Fell from the Sky: A Disappearance, a Daughter's Search, and Cambodia's First War Criminal*

"*Troubling the Water* is a haunting and lyrical eulogy to Cambodia's once magnificent Tonle Sap Lake and the water culture of Cambodia. With precise reporting Abby Seiff reveals how centuries of rich fishing and abundant water have been depleted, replaced by an emerging dystopia. Chinese dams choked off water from the Mekong River while Cambodia's corrupt government exploited the lake's riches, leaving the Tonle Sap defenseless against the droughts, dry winds, and extreme weather of the climate crisis. Seiff's is an important addition to the literature on our planet's global warming."

—ELIZABETH BECKER, author of *You Don't Belong Here: How Three Women Rewrote the Story of War*

"Abby Seiff's groundbreaking book deals with one of the most important and disturbing ecological issues facing mainland Southeast Asia. Little noticed away from Cambodia, that country's great lake, the Tonle Sap, is being dramatically degraded as a consequence of dams built by China on the Mekong River, climate change, and destructive human activity. There are now doubts that the Tonle Sap can continue to act as the essential source of fish, the key source of protein in the Cambodian population's diet. The author exposes the human costs of this development with empathy and a deep understanding of the issues involved."

—MILTON OSBORNE, author of *The Mekong: Turbulent Past, Uncertain Future*

"The destruction of human life can occur slowly, indirectly, and even imperceptibly, which makes it no less of a crime. When natural resources supporting human life are maliciously destroyed in a similar manner and on such a great scale, there is no difference than committing a crime against humanity. This book reminds us of how much our humanity is connected to our environment."

—YOUK CHHANG, founder and executive director of Documentation Center of Cambodia and executive producer of *A River Changes Course*

TROUBLING THE WATER

TROUBLING

THE WATER

A Dying Lake and a Vanishing World in Cambodia

ABBY SEIFF

POTOMAC BOOKS   *An imprint of the University of Nebraska Press*

Portions of this book were previously published as "In
Cambodia, Holdouts Fight a Rising Tide," Devex,
August 3, 2017, https://www.devex.com/news/in
-cambodia-holdouts-fight-a-rising-tide-90789; "In
the Mekong, Questions Arise over Impact of Favoring
Hydropower," Devex, April 11, 2018, https://www
.devex.com/news/in-the-mekong-questions-arise
-over-impact-of-favoring-hydropower-92384; "The
Tonle Sap," *Mekong Review*, November 2020, https://
mekongreview.com/the-tonle-sap/; "The Water
People," *Mekong Review*, February 2018, https://
mekongreview.com/the-water-people/; and "When
There Are No More Fish," Eater and Vox Media, LLC,
December 29, 2017, https://www.eater.com/2017
/12/29/16823664/tonle-sap-drought-cambodia.

Library of Congress Cataloging-in-Publication Data
Names: Seiff, Abby, author.
Title: Troubling the water : a dying lake and a
vanishing world in Cambodia / Abby Seiff.
Description: [Lincoln, NE] : Potomac Books, an imprint
of the University of Nebraska Press, [2022] |
Includes bibliographical references and index.
Identifiers: LCCN 2021035776
ISBN 9781640124769 (paperback)
ISBN 9781640125247 (eub)
ISBN 9781640125254 (pdf)
Subjects: LCSH: Tonle Sap (Cambodia : Lake) |
Water resources development—Cambodia. | Water-
supply—Cambodia—Management. | BISAC:
NATURE / Ecosystems & Habitats / Rivers | SOCIAL
SCIENCE / Ethnic Studies / Asian Studies
Classification: LCC HD1698.C36 T76
2022 | DDC 333.91009596—dc23
LC record available at https://lccn.loc.gov/2021035776

Set in Adobe Garamond by Laura Buis.
Designed by N. Putens.

To Mom and Dad

Pull the boat without leaving tracks; catch fish without troubling the water.

—CAMBODIAN PROVERB

CONTENTS

ILLUSTRATIONS

A NOTE ON TRANSLATIONS

Several excellent interpreters assisted me during fieldwork for this book. Chhorn Chansy and Seng Sophea contributed the most, translating for me during reporting trips on and around the Tonle Sap. Heng Sokharany translated at the villages surrounding the Lower Sesan 2 dam; Len Leng translated in Koh Preah; Neou Vannarin translated a poem; and Mech Dara conducted additional interviews in 2020. Translation requires so much more than simply substituting one language in for another, and I am immensely grateful for the care each interpreter took to put sources at ease, navigate cross-cultural difficulties, provide insightful context, and put up with my barang fumbling. I am extremely fortunate to have these colleagues, and it goes without saying that any errors in this text are entirely my own.

TROUBLING THE WATER

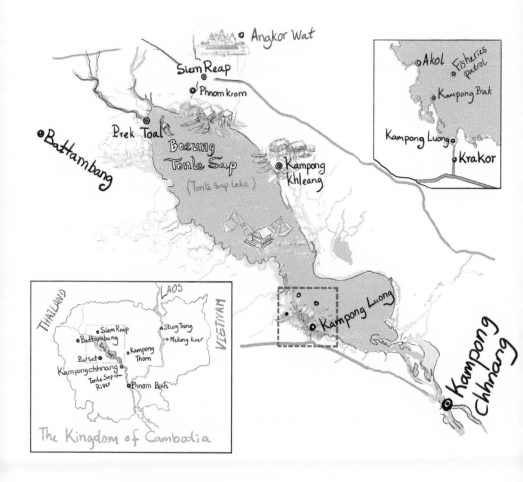

MAP I. The Tonle Sap Lake. Courtesy of Sao Sreymao.

PROLOGUE

A prince from a distant land traveled across the water for many days. Exhausted, he alighted on an island and fell asleep. The underworld beneath him seethed with powerful gods. Among them, a beauty: the daughter of the Naga king. The Naga were serpentine and amphibious. They moved between water and land, human and animal. When the human prince and the Naga princess married, the king blessed their union by drinking the ocean. Land emerged, a gift to the couple. The land born of water was Cambodia.

There is a yellowed map of Cambodia hanging on my wall in New York. It's a 1:100,000-scale map with Phnom Penh spidering out from the center. A tiny knot of busy city lines fades into the rural lands that comprise most of the country to this day. Low-lying floodplains sit to the west, south, and north of Phnom Penh. To the east are the rivers that made this city a trade center hundreds of years before it became Cambodia's capital.

The four river arms look like a messy X, with Phnom Penh nestled where they cross. The Mekong River is a fat line, carving in from the northeast before abruptly doglegging at the confluence and spilling southeast toward the delta in Vietnam. A slimmer tributary, the Bassac River, pulls off from the Mekong and flows south, nearly parallel to its mother river. The Tonle Sap River is the fourth arm, cleaved from the Mekong to drift its way northwest. On this map, you can trace the turquoise line up only fifty miles and so you can't see how the Tonle Sap River slices toward the Tonle Sap Lake, spilling into the huge basin that cuts across the nation's center.

You can't see how that river expands and contracts with the seasons, either. It's just a static line.

The map is in Vietnamese—a relic of the ten years of occupation after the fall of the Khmer Rouge—and I bought it shortly after I first moved to Phnom Penh, at what is widely called the Russian Market (another hint of the complex geopolitics that have jostled this small country over the course of its history). I arrived in 2009 to work as a reporter at an English-language newspaper, the *Cambodia Daily*, and stayed to edit at the *Phnom Penh Post*, and then stayed longer still, working as a freelance journalist. I made some of the deepest relationships of my life and did some of the hardest work it seemed I might ever encounter and experienced some of my finest regrets. I moved home, briefly. I moved to Bangkok, briefly. I moved to Melbourne, briefly. In between, I seemed unable to stop boomeranging back to Phnom Penh.

I moved house nine times in four countries between when I bought the map and when I returned to New York in 2019. Each time, I unfolded it carefully along those browning lines, the fine paper snowing from my fingers, and tacked it near my desk. It was like a talisman, this map, a reminder of how complicated and special things could be.

When the Dominican missionary Gabriel Quiroga de San Antonio first laid his eyes on the Tonle Sap Lake in the late 1590s, so confounded was he by its size that he assumed he must still be on the mighty Mekong. The "magnificently built" city of Angkor—with its fortified stone wall, its coats of arms, mysterious lettering, and Roman-style porticos—lies "on the shore of the Mekhong." The "river," he wrote, is "subject to swelling and subsidence. The tide makes itself felt more than one hundred and seventy leagues from there, its waters feed a lot of fish."[1]

How to explain the inexorable link between water and culture in Cambodia? Imagine a classical dancer, fingers fanning a fluid wave up through her elbow, face still as a lake. The movement, handed down from one royal court to another, echoes that of the *apsaras* gliding across the lintels of Angkor Wat. Where did these celestial spirits of cloud and rain come from? They were born of yet more water, when the sea of milk was churned by gods and demons, coming together to create the elixir of immortality, ready to make and unmake the world.

At the height of its power, in the 1200s, Angkor was a city of one million people. (London at the time had a population of around forty-five thousand.) Today, archaeologists use low-flying planes and lasers to trace Angkor's contours. On their maps, a network of waterways branch out clean as those on any modern city grid. They carve from the temples to the Tonle Sap Lake and from massive man-made reservoirs toward the mountains. Here is the underpinning of the city's vast hydrological system, which tamed the water with such success as to support an empire. Is it any wonder that Angkor's walls are covered with boats and fish and the epic tale of an ocean churned?

Neither can you divide the water nor can you cut off flesh from flesh, a Khmer proverb warns. *The water rises, the fish eat the ants. The water recedes, the ant eats the fish,* consoles another. *Pull the boat without leaving tracks, catch fish without troubling the water.*[2]

Some proverbs stretch into folktales. Some folktales stretch into stories. The first modern novel in Cambodia told a sensational tale of marriage and justice, love and loss, attempted murder and retribution. Published in three installments in 1939, Kim Hak's book recalls Buddhist precepts, Cambodian legends, and high drama. Its name? *Dik Danle Sap*, "The waters of the Tonle Sap." The book reflects back the most traditional of Khmer literature—a story of black and white, good and evil, ogres and princes—in novel form. The titular lake exerts its own power: sweeping people away, bringing them together, changing human lives as the waters follow their natural course.[3]

The river confluence where Phnom Penh sits is known as *chaktomuk*, or four faces. Where those four river branches meet is a holy site: the royal palace sits near here, and here, too, swim the ashes of kings and queens, scattered upon their deaths. There is an exquisite theater here, built by Vann Molyvann, Cambodia's foremost modern architect. Its name is Chaktomuk.

The city's riverfront skates behind the theater, past a holy shrine, the city's oldest pagoda, and sleepy lines of art deco apartments. Concrete steps lead down to the water. Watch them disappear, once the rains come and swell the river. At the height of the dry season, around February or March, you can stand here and watch a line emerge at the center of the confluence: a still, brown Tonle Sap on the near side cleaving neatly from the swift, blue Mekong. Come November, as the rainy season draws to a close, one million people converge at this spot for the Water Festival. There are concerts, fireworks, and parties. There are grand perambulations around the capital for those who have never seen such city madness in their lives. There are fun fairs set up along the riverbanks. There are royal floats lit by thousands of tiny lights, set adrift, blazing, as the sun drops.

And then, of course, there are the races: the true raison d'être of the festival. Scores of rowers cram into slim dragon boats that look scarcely different from those on the walls of Angkor. The boats, some holding as many as one hundred scullers, sit so low in the river it seems a wonder they can move, let alone race. Oars churn at the water and the boats fling forward, down the Tonle Sap River, toward the confluence, toward victory.

After months of rain, the river is no longer the yellowed, low-lying stillness of dry season. Now it is turbulent and swift. And the races, the floats, the fireworks, and the concerts are here to celebrate this singular fact: the river has reversed course.

When a hard rain comes, the lake undulates. One morning in May 2016, at the start of the rainy season, I watched as a storm battered the Tonle Sap. Only puffed-candy clouds hung in the sky, but the sun shower came like a monsoon, sending flat waves skittering across the surface of the lake. In front of me, boaters pressed on. A trio of drenched women sent a slim wood pirogue forward, slowly, on slender oars. A man jetted past on a lime-green longboat, propeller cutting neatly across the silvered skin of the water. For hours, the air had grown heavier and here was the release. Small patches of water hyacinth unmoored by the wind followed the current out. Across the way, a shopkeeper rearranged her stock.

A long dry season was ending, and with it, the worst drought in years. It was the drought that brought me to the lake. I had come to report on its impact, and rain—its lateness, its absence—was on everyone's mind. This shower came with the force of a gasp and I ducked into an empty school for shelter. Behind me, three little boys ran laughing through the classrooms, soaked and enraptured. The downpour stopped after just thirty minutes. By the time I boated inland a few hours later, the banks along the lake were bone-dry once again, embroidered with dry-season cracks.

When the rains finally came in full, the lake would overspill the banks and forests lining it, transforming Cambodia's topography. Over the course of the rainy season, the Tonle Sap expands up to six times in area. It covers nearly a tenth of the country in water that comes no higher than the toes, the ankles, the calves. Viewed from above, it seems an ocean has swallowed Cambodia.

The school where I sat would be floated inland, following the water line. The boaters, whose homes were now perched on a muddy bank, would lash their floors to plastic drums and bamboo poles and let them rise with the water. The trees would shrink, the jungle made over as a floating forest, the trunks used as anchors for floating homes.

Beneath our feet, the underworld would seethe. Millions of fish would gather near the roots of the submerged trees to feast on a slurry of nutrients, mate, and lay eggs. Minerals would weep from the lake's center, soaking into the soil and up the paddy rice. The world around us would become fecund and rich.

And then, just as surely, the rains would stop and the lake would wrinkle back inward; the ocean consumed once again by the land.

The Tonle Sap system lies near the bottom of the nearly three-thousand-mile-long Mekong, which is among the longest and most prodigious rivers in the world. After the Amazon, the Mekong basin is the globe's second most biodiverse. It is the biggest inland fishery and contains more large fish than any other river.

Myriad tributaries spill from the Mekong, but few are as essential as the Tonle Sap River, which holds a crucial ecological link to the larger system. Twice a year, the Tonle Sap reverses course, the only river on earth to do so. The first reversal typically takes place in May, as the new monsoon rains flood the Mekong. The influx of water is so strong and fast, its excess courses into the Tonle Sap River, pushing at it until it reverses course entirely and sends water up to the Tonle Sap Lake. About six months later, at the end of rainy season, dropping Mekong water levels see the river reverse course once again—the lake pours its water out into the Tonle Sap River, which flows back toward the Mekong.

Scientists call that a monotonal flood-pulsed system; poets liken it to a beating heart. That pulsation has made the lake into the world's most extraordinary fish basin and has created an extremely fertile floodplain.

The Tonle Sap Lake is the largest body of freshwater in all of Southeast Asia, but next to the world's biggest lakes, Cambodia's is a pond. At its biggest, the volume of Tonle Sap is about eighteen cubic miles; more than sixty-five such lakes could fit into Lake Michigan. Its maximum depth is about forty-five feet, while Lake Victoria (considered a shallow lake) bottoms out at 270. What makes Tonle Sap so remarkable, then? Its prodigious spread, swelled by the flood pulse. During rainy season, the surface area of the lake reaches about six thousand square miles, nearly the size of Fiji.

"The double movement of the lake, the annual pulsation of this gigantic heart connected with the thousand arteries of the Mekong, is the life of the fishermen," the French explorer Lieutenant Jules Marcel Brossard de Corbigny observed in 1871.[4]

The system is a finely tuned ecological miracle. Pull a single thread and it will begin unraveling. We, as it turns out, are pulling all its threads at once.

Today, dams, climate change, and overfishing are rapidly unmaking the Tonle Sap Lake and the larger Mekong basin. Deforestation is sending soil plummeting into the floodplains, changing their composition. Silt is being blocked by dams, depleting necessary nutrients from the paddy fields. Fish are disappearing from the lake, meaning they are also disappearing from the higher reaches of the Mekong River. Stupendous amounts of water are being held back by the hydropower dams strung along the Mekong's mainstem, sending its water level plummeting. In turn, the water volume of the lake drops lower by the year, and the reversal of the Tonle Sap River comes later.

One day soon, the river will likely stop reversing course and the Tonle Sap Lake, for all intents and purposes, will die.

In the dry season, the stilted villages stop floating. I drove to one on a gray dawn in March 2017, moving from urban sprawl, past factories, and a wide expanse of farmland. Underfoot, the road changed from tarmac to packed red dirt, and the houses thinned out before thickening once more as we neared the Tonle Sap. We pulled up to an inlet leading to the lake, where homes bumped against one another, towering twenty feet up on their spindly legs. Life thrummed in the spaces below. An infant napped in a hammock, impervious to the children careening past; shrimp traps hung from the rafters like bunches of grapes; a family repaired torn fishing nets, squinting as they tied off fresh knots.

When there is no water, all action takes place under the shade of the houses. Aunties had set up their shops there, fat orange coolers and neat cigarette displays at the ready. A rooster pecked at some crumbs. Under one house, neighborhood women—hired day laborers—cleaned pound after pound of tiny fish at enormous speed.

Behind the houses lay a graveyard of dusty, broken boats: a speedboat without its motor, a houseboat missing its arched shelter. Fishers streamed along the inlet to the lake, sending a wave of silver-gray water lapping at its pockmarked banks. Twenty minutes, more, before they would make it to the lip, and farther, still, until they could cast those newly mended nets. The lake drifts inland slower and slower and the trip lengthens by the year. When the lake pulsed out, at last, though, this inlet would disappear, as would the roads. The rooster and his bamboo dome would be moved skyward. The boats would be tied to those limblike stilts; no need to drag them up the bank. Stairs would lead into the water and the undersides of the homes would be transformed into lake. Each house mirrored, wobbly, in the wet below.

Across the globe, just 2.5 percent of our water is fresh and most of that is locked away in ice. All of the lakes, rivers, wetlands, and ponds combined make up barely 1 percent of freshwater. That tiny fraction of accessible freshwater, .007 percent of the planet's water, is what sustains our life. It is the source of our drinking water and the means with which we grow our food. And that water alone supports half of all species of fish.

Researchers have only begun to understand the extent and importance of inland, freshwater fisheries like the Tonle Sap. Known as "hidden harvest," the global inland fish catch may be underreported by as much as 65 percent.[5] Nearly all of that catch is happening in low-income countries, carried out by sustenance fishers. In many of those places, fish is the main source of protein. We are losing these bodies of water at a rapid clip, and we barely understand what an enormous amount of food each one is providing. Large freshwater species are at the brink of extinction, having declined 94 percent since 1970.[6]

Lake Victoria and the Aral Sea; the Amazon basin and the Great Lakes—all have faced deep environmental devastation in recent decades that has destroyed native fish populations, with catastrophic results for the surrounding human populations. The most threatened group of vertebrates on earth is now believed to be freshwater fish.

In Cambodia, the flood pulse is responsible for the Tonle Sap's fish. Its failure spells disaster. Billions of fish representing more than two hundred species migrate from the Mekong through the Tonle Sap River and into the lake. Across the globe, only a handful of countries—all many times the size of Cambodia—boast larger inland fisheries. But few rely on their lakes to the extent that Cambodia does. The fish, some five hundred thousand tons of which are caught each year, feed the nation, providing the primary protein for as much as 80 percent of the population.

The tremors on the lake are felt far beyond its banks. The slowing pulse upends fish migration patterns, pulling species not just from the lake but from across the Mekong and its tributaries. The combined catch of the lake and the rest of the lower Mekong's fisheries provides 15 percent of global inland fish production—more than any other location on the planet.[7] The impact is reaching other food sources, too. In Cambodia, a static lake means little water reaches the rice paddy fields surrounding the Tonle Sap. Downstream, as the flood pulse diminishes, with it goes an annual surge of Mekong water responsible for a third of the delta's freshwater supply. Encroaching seawater is now killing off the fertile basin responsible for half of Vietnam's rice crop, a significant portion of which is exported across the globe.

As the fish disappear from the Tonle Sap, the livelihoods of millions are being destroyed. On the lake, an entire way of life is vanishing as fishers scatter to pursue risky jobs at factories, construction sites, and plantations. The debt burden is mounting to dangerous levels. In many ways, the situation at the lake is a harbinger of what is to come in countries both rich and poor, as rapacious development consumes society's most vulnerable communities.

How is a system that worked with such precision, for such a long time, unmade so quickly? This, sadly, is not particularly complicated to answer. Greed and mismanagement, confused priorities and petty corruption, and the tragedy of the commons have all conspired to damn the Tonle Sap. But what does it mean for those who rely on the lake? What does it mean to lose a way of living that sustained families for centuries? These are the questions that began poking at me several years ago.

In 2016 I took my first reporting trip to the lake. It was a very bad drought year and my friend, photographer Nicolas Axelrod, wanted to document the situation there. We went to Siem Reap with Seng Sophea, a Cambodian tour guide and translator, and began making our way around the lake: driving to the stilt villages hugging its cracked edges and boating through channels to visit homes floating on calf-high water.

We spoke with fishers and officials, with fish buyers and shop owners, with kids and the elderly. Everyone told us the same thing: the water was lower than ever, the fish were smaller than ever, there seemed to be almost none left in the lake. In village after village, residents showed us the empty houses where former inhabitants had left for Thailand or to work at a factory in the city. "It's changed so much," people would say, pointing to a dry river or a patch of lake: "When I was young, I could scoop fish out of there with a basket."

I had been writing about Cambodia's uneven, breakneck development since I first arrived. Such stories were not new to me. But the lake encapsulated all this in a particularly tragic, maddening way. Here we are, watching this disappear before our eyes, knowing the impact and doing nothing.

Early the next year, Nick and I returned with an environmental researcher, Areeya Tivasuradej, and with my friend Chhorn Chansy, then an editor at the *Cambodia Daily*.

We went to some of the same communities and visited new ones. The 2017 catch was better but the overall situation was little improved. Everyone was in debt; lots of people were still being forced to migrate for work; no one expected their kids to grow up to be fishers. There was, increasingly, a sense that this very way of life had come to an end. The fishers graciously discussed their troubles. They spoke to us inside their homes, from their boats, or standing, mid-catch, in the water. When we asked where the fish went, they told us the same things: illegal fishing, climate change, dams. When we asked what could be done, some shrugged and said it was just the way it was; but most suggested better enforcement of the laws or government assistance. If outsiders may have romanticized their lost way of life, the fishers were practical. Give us farmland, give us a better opportunity, they offered.

After those early trips, I began researching descriptions of the lake. They are everywhere, when you start to look. The Chinese, the Spanish, the Portuguese, and the French all sent explorers and emissaries and rank colonialists to Cambodia. Anyone who made it up to the Tonle Sap was invariably taken by the "freshwater sea." The remarkable fishery features in proverbs and art; it features on the walls of Angkor; it even features in the fossilized remains of two-thousand-year-old meals.

I returned again later that year and the interviews by then had become like a rhythm: there are no more fish; we can't stay here; we have nowhere else to go.

On the one hand, fish were still being pulled in and exported. The Water Festival was still sending boaters battling against the current. Tourists were still flocking to the floating villages and stilt homes speckling the Tonle Sap.

On the other, 2019 was the worst drought year yet. Chinese dams on the upper part of the Mekong switched off the tap.[8] The water in the Mekong dropped to a historic low. The Tonle Sap River reversed course two months late. The pulse had almost stopped.

By then I had moved home to New York. Watching this from afar felt sickening. My friends in Southeast Asia sent me haunting photos and charts. Nick went back to the lake and said the situation had grown dire. "Every time I go back I have less and less hope," he texted.

Another year passed. The coronavirus pandemic tore through the country's delicate economy in 2020. Halts to global manufacturing and free movement shredded its garment industry and tourism sector, the two cornerstones supporting the country. On the lake, families who relied heavily on remittances faced a second blow. Technically, the Tonle Sap River reversed course in August—three months late—but it didn't really reverse until October, when flash floods finally sent the water pouring in earnest back toward the lake. The water level of the lake hit another historic low, reaching just a quarter of its normal wet season volume. Officials were calling it a "very critical situation."[9] Fishers had predicted in 2016 the Tonle Sap might survive another ten to twenty years. But it had become clear it was dying before our eyes.

It is hopeless at times, but it is not *only* hopeless. There are many brave, inventive people carving lives from the margins—though it must be said that far many more are slipping through the cracks through no fault of their own. So much could be done to help them and to mitigate against the worst of the catastrophe. If it is too late to turn back the clock and restore the Tonle Sap, as I fear it may be, let this be some small attempt to memorialize a place and time before it vanishes.

1 *The Tiger Depends on the Forest*

Charred forest has a curious smell. Sweet and acrid, both, the soil somehow purer, the air wood-rich. In May 2016 the forest at the northern tip of the Tonle Sap isn't razed to the ground; trees still stand in sliding lines against a baby-cloud sky. But they are mostly blackened skeletons, leaves turned dust in the recent conflagration. A small river leads from the lake through the protected wetlands of Prek Toal. Fire has transformed its landscape.

For months now, blazes have been stalking across the flooded forests rimming the lake. These are unprecedented occurrences. I talk to people in their fifties, sixties, and seventies, and no one has seen this kind of thing before. Wildfires, so common in the rest of the world, are rarities in Cambodia's flooded forests. But here they have come, flames blowing high, sparks jumping from one dry patch to the next—all near the largest body of fresh water in Southeast Asia. By the time they burn out, the fires have reached a third of the Tonle Sap's forests and wetlands, damaging hundreds of square miles and killing countless animals.[1]

Chang Laom is my guide through this erased land. She is tiny and voluble, with a half-grin that pulls the wrinkles from her neck and cheeks. Laom pats my arm as she marches us forward, even as small fires still smoke farther in. It looks like charcoal under foot, a fine layer of pure black coating the red soil. It's so dry here that clumps of dirt have pulled apart in jagged circles and squares. A few green shoots push up, improbably, through the cracked earth. Tall golden stalks of grass and reeds catch at the faint breeze; a mess of twigs are tangled above the blackened ground.

"I don't know why it is so hot and dry. I've never seen that before. I'm sixty-six and this is the first time I ever saw these fires," she says.

When we turn back from the forest, crossing the land where it shears from the fire line, I see that a section of her garden has been spared the flames. It is a strange sight: the strong young plants, leafy and full set against molting trees. There's a thin fence around some seedlings, lines of old fishing netting held up by sticks. She points out where she has sown new crops. "I started to plant some vegetables again. I don't know if they will grow."

At the edge of Laom's garden stands a blackened tree with a crown of coppered leaves, wrapped with the bright green of a vine untouched by the blaze. Twenty feet in front of us, her small wood house lists on its stilts. Another ten feet ahead, the water hits the shore.

"I've lived here for more than thirty years and have never seen a fire here in my life. It started from the canal over there, then the wind brought it here. It lasted two days. We used water pumps to try and stop it but it wasn't enough," Laom says.

While Laom speaks, she smooths her clothes, orange chains wrapping across the indigo leaves of her skirt. A soft patch of pumpkin plants furl away from Laom, their butter-yellow flowers catching at the sun.

For days, neighbors gathered at this river, dragging hoses and motorized pumps from home to home to keep the flames at bay. Monks joined, and officers, the more able-bodied among them moving deeper into the forest, which is an important bird sanctuary. What is a small hose to an inferno? "The speed and power was like gas burning," one neighbor recounts. Birds fell from the sky as in some dark tale. That the waterside houses and gardens had been spared at all spoke to the superhuman effort. "All of the villagers came to help," Laom's husband, Seng Kimluon, tells me. "If we hadn't, the whole village would have burned."

But now the woods are crumbling, and Laom wonders what will happen once the water begins to rise with the rainy season and the houses are readied to float inland with the lake.

"In the wet season, we move to this area and tie our houses to the trees—everyone here does that," she says, gesturing at the splintering forest behind her.

"If this tree is still alive I can tie my home during wet season. If it's dead, I can't."

At the end of the thirteenth century, a Chinese emissary named Zhou Daguan traveled to the majestic city of Angkor set on the Tonle Sap, which he termed a "Freshwater Sea." Here, he penned the oldest known outsider's account of life among the sprawling palaces and temples, among tidy villages and lush paddy fields. In his colorful *A Record of Cambodia: The Land and Its People*, he wrote of the seasons, of how life changes on the lake.

At the height of the monsoon, he noted, "the high water mark around the Freshwater Sea can reach some seventy or eighty feet, completely submerging even very tall trees except for the tips. Families living by the shore all move to the far side of the hills." When the lake contracts with the dry season, "only small boats can cross the Sea, whose lower depths are no more than three to five feet down. The families move back down again, and the farmers work out when the paddy will be ripe and when the waters will have spread where, and sow their seed accordingly."[2]

The dry season can be hot, unbearably so, but it remains part of the natural order. Drought is something different. In 2016 Southeast Asia faced one of the worst droughts in recorded history. Tens of thousands of acres of crops were destroyed, rivers dried up, and health problems flourished. A massive El Niño, which started in the middle of 2015 and followed a lesser 2014 El Niño, put an early end to the rainy season and sent temperatures soaring across the region. In Cambodia, fish exports plummeted 21 percent.[3]

Near the equator, trade winds in the Pacific send ocean currents and warm water westwards. During an El Niño, those winds slow and warm water is sent back east. In a La Niña, the trade winds grow stronger, and cool jet streams develop. Depending on the season, these events can lead to drier or wetter than average conditions and increases in hurricanes, droughts, and other natural disasters. El Niños and La Niñas are normal weather patterns—their regular arrival observed and recorded for centuries. But scientists believe they have been exacerbated by climate change and are arriving more frequently and with greater strength.[4] Much of Cambodia's population relies on subsistence farming and fishing, and the country is routinely ranked among those most vulnerable to climate change. The low water and cracked paddy fields caused by an El Niño have repercussions for millions.

One toll of climate change is extreme weather at either end: higher highs, lower lows. In the coming years, it is expected that both droughts and flooding will worsen. The temperature of the Earth in 2016 was the warmest on record. Nearly every year since has seen some new global high. The past five years have been the five warmest on record, part of a decade of "exceptional heat."[5]

In the Mekong, the droughts—coupled with rampant hydropower damming—have contributed to repeated, grim milestones. In 2010 the Mekong dipped to its lowest levels since modern recording began, only to surpass that low in 2016, and then again in 2019.

Without enough water volume in the Mekong, the Tonle Sap River can't reverse course and the lake stays shallow, its floodplains dry. Without the pulse, there is no water for the rice paddies surrounding the Tonle Sap. The stagnation changes how fish migrate and nutrients move. What is left of the lake?

In both Hindu and Buddhist mythology, Mount Meru sits at the center of the universe, home to the gods who rule the world below. This universe lies in the middle of the Cosmic Ocean—the origin of everything.

When the Angkorian king Indravarman I came to power in 877, he built a reservoir. "In five days, I will begin to dig," read an inscription describing the vow he made upon his coronation.[6] When his son, Yasovarman I, ascended the throne, he built another reservoir. In the early eleventh century, Suryavarman I started construction of the biggest hand cut reservoir in the world, even today. Rajendravarman II built reservoirs. Jayavarman VII built reservoirs. King after king built reservoir after reservoir. Angkor Wat, Phnom Bakheng, Banteay Srei, Bayon—temples—are what these rulers are most famous for. But the massive man-made lakes left no less of a legacy. If the sumptuous temples of Angkor represent Mount Meru, the reservoirs are its Cosmic Ocean: billions of gallons of water for the making of a new world. The king, the one who built it all, was a god on earth.

Tourists who visit Angkor Archaeological Park today can see scores of striking temples and monuments across 150 square miles. That is only a fraction of the city's historic size. At its peak, in the twelfth century, Angkor spanned more than 380 square miles.

In 2010 a group of archaeologists began crisscrossing the skies north of the lake in helicopters, aiming lasers at the site of the former Angkorian city.[7] Lidar surveying uses pulsing light to measure distance, helping researchers create unprecedented renderings of ancient sites. Where farmland and forest have overrun those contours, lidar can draw a map of urban sprawl that hasn't been seen fully for centuries.

What these maps show at a glance is water: moats surround towers; reservoirs, large and small, stud the land; canals cut in neat north-south and east-west lines, snake across a grid. A number of small stone structures sit inside the moat surrounding the complex's most famous temple, Angkor Wat. Archaeologists now believe there were homes in the inner complexes of many of the temples—thousands of wood structures housing the huge population. In the lidar map, every single one of those homes sits alongside its own personal reservoir.[8]

The French archaeologist Bernard Philippe Groslier was the first to coin the term *la cité hydraulique angkorienne*, in the 1960s, but its waterways wouldn't have gone unnoticed by those living in the area.[9] The West Baray—a massive reservoir totaling more than six square miles and holding billions of gallons of water—is used by farmers to this day. A stick-straight, fifteen-mile north channel runs down from nearby hills to the gates of Angkor Thom. The remains of smaller reservoirs dot Siem Reap's countryside.

The complex water management system utilized the Tonle Sap Lake and a trio of rivers that spilled from the nearby Kulen Mountain, collecting and draining in turn.[10] Massive reservoirs were a symbol of a king's divinity and generosity. They reflected his place in the cosmic system and may well have provided irrigation and drinking water, the means to grow a city.[11]

For hundreds of years, this system worked flawlessly. The lake and the waterways offered abundant fish and a reliable means of transportation and connectivity. Whereas many Cambodian farmers today struggle to annually grow one good crop of rice, Angkorian farmers planted as often as three times a year.

As in Cambodia's origin story, the water covered the lands and the gods tamed the water.

But humans and gods alike are prone to hubris. The legends show us, too, how our folly will cut us down time and time again.

The rings from thousand-year-old trees tell the story of repeated, extreme droughts running from the middle of the fourteenth to the early fifteenth centuries.[12] Punctuated by severe monsoons, these droughts undid much of Angkor. The reservoirs and canals dried up. When the water returned, it came with a violent force that flooded and damaged the critical network, rendering it unusable. Soil erosion, hastened by the felling of forests to make way for the city, silted up the channels. By the end of the fourteenth century, the royal court moved elsewhere and the population shrank. Before long, the Angkorian kingdom ceased to exist.

Downriver from Chang Laom's house sits Ly Heng's shop, abutting its own section of charred forest. His store is packed with every conceivable item a Prek Toal resident could need: baby powder and fans, sealant and birth control, a new red dress and a saw, a propeller and a bottle of yellow nail polish.

Behind the shop are a series of shack-sized wood-and-chicken-wire cages full of crocodiles. This is business number two. Rubbery crocodile eggs are stored in one cage; baby crocs no longer than a forearm waddle across another. The biggest crocs, longer than a man, live in a massive penned-in area farther back toward the forest. They cool themselves in a concrete pond and rest in dusty heaps beneath the sawed plank walkways that run the length of their enclosure. When Heng feeds them, throwing fish down from his wooden perch, they writhe on top of one another, jaws snapping open to reveal startlingly yellow tongues.

Crocs are a booming business on the lake, bred and raised for eight years before they are exported to Vietnam, Thailand, and China—or sold to local factories that turn their nubby skin into midrange purses and shoes sold at tourist shops across Siem Reap city. It's not a cheap endeavor but it's a fairly easy growth business. As the fires surged forward, Heng wondered if his entire farm could be lost in a moment.

"We went into the jungle and tried to stop it but we couldn't," he says. "Many hectares were burning everywhere. We had some help from the government's environmental officers, but it was impossible to stop it. It was a huge fire and we just had a small tube to pump water."

The flames burned out at last, sating themselves on the forest without moving on to consume the homes, the shops, and the crocodiles—some miracle. But their effect would linger.

"Since the time of my ancestors, there had never been a forest fire. I think if the temperature keeps getting hotter and hotter it will happen again," Heng says, his voice resigned.

The village of Kok Ai moves with the rains, but in 2016 there isn't enough water to travel on. It is late May—it should have been raining for a month now, filling the lake and its inlets, covering the land. Instead, the area is too dry, smoke still curling up in the distance. Fuel is running low, as are supplies, and the catch is nearly worthless. Many are going hungry: Here! On the water! When fish should have been everywhere! One woman is heavily pregnant. Will she make it off the lake in time? Usually, the residents would already be dismantling their camp and starting to boat upstream, back to their land-life. But everything is moving at a different pace this year. Worry threads through the village, a thick, rich vein of fear.

About fifty Cham Muslim families make up Kok Ai. They've set up camp on a broad patch of land near to where Battambang's Sangke River spills into the northern tip of the Tonle Sap. They come here to fish for just four months. It's nearing the end and the camp looks rough: A thin layer of trash—soda cans and medicine bottles, foil wrappers and straws—are scattered like fallen leaves. The homes here are made from forest materials: skinny branches stabbed into the ground, covered with thatch. Only a fortunate few have plastic rolled out over the roof. A dwindling number of ducks and chickens peck at the ground beneath their bamboo enclosures.

For days, the fires stalked this bank. Just across the narrow waterway lie grasslands—an emerald swath freckled with charred shrubs. The rust and black of burned wood press against an odd, impossibly green bush. The width of the water, the turn of the breeze, had somehow spared the camp.

"We were really shocked and scared the fire would come over here. The flames were so high and there was a lot of ash falling," Tinh Pas recounts, just a few days after the worst of it had passed. "Most of the jungle was on fire. Some animals were killed." Birds tore out of the forest, taking flight before flailing and crashing into the water, into the boats.

In all my time in Cambodia, I have come across few people living in more dire straits than those at Kok Ai. None have homes—no money for that. They shuffle up and down the river, packing their belongings into small boats, dismantling and resurrecting their lives four times each year. When the fishing season is over, Kok Ai residents work in construction or in brick making—a dangerous profession reserved exclusively for Cambodia's most destitute and desperate. During the months these villagers camp on the lake, the aim is to pull in as much fish as possible. They eat and preserve some of what they catch, and they sell the rest to a middleman. In this way, they may scrape by. But in 2016 there are just no fish.

"It's a big difference from last year," says Los Rokeas. She is forty-eight and has been following this double movement all her life. The current situation is remarkable and ruinous. "Every year I can do some fishing. Not now. Some people can't even afford to eat. We're almost broke because the water is completely dry."

She takes me inside her home, a broad, low structure with a swept dirt floor. Clothes hang from the rafters and there's a raised wood platform in the back, for sleeping, eating, and keeping the food dry. The floor is a dull brown, the thatching bleached blond, the rafters worn bamboo, but Rokeas is pure color. A cobalt headscarf sits high on her forehead, pulling out the blue from a top riddled with flowers. Her skirt is bright purple, patterned with gold stars and curlicues. She holds her baby grand-daughter, dressed in a frilly, black-checked top and pink-flower pants, in the curve of her lap. A tiny bracelet circles her wrist.

"We want to go back, but it's impossible to access the river because the water is so low. Every year we go back around now but this month we're stuck," says Rokeas.

Her friend Tinh Pas interjects: "Yesterday, we couldn't go fishing at all because it was completely dry."

"Since I was young, I've come here," says Rokeas. "Usually, we would catch ten or twenty kilos. Now, we only catch around two kilos each day to sell to the businessmen who come up here. Sometimes we spend more on gasoline than we earn."

Another woman wanders over, offers her take.

"We can't do anything anymore. We can't make enough to get rice to eat."

Rokeas directs us to look at the crumbling camp surrounding us. She points out a shallow wicker basket where a handful of small fish are curing in the relentless sun, their flesh slowly changing into a durable food. "Every year lots of fish would be drying here. Now you see only one basket."

The French naturalist Henri Mouhot wondered if the shape of the Tonle Sap might be compared to a violin.[13] When he reached the lake, in December 1859, the waters would have already begun to recede—shrinking back from the floodplains, revealing all those hidden roads and trees.

"The entrance" to the lake, he wrote, "is grand and beautiful. The river becomes wider and wider, until at last it is four or five miles in breadth; and then you enter the immense sheet of water called Touli-Sap, as large and full of motion as a sea . . . The waves glitter in the broad sunshine with a brilliancy which the eye can scarcely support, and, in many parts of the lake, nothing is visible all around but water."

At the time, the Tonle Sap was cleaved in half. In the center, signposts demarcated the border between Siam and Cambodia. North of that line, Thai authorities held control. At Cambodia's eastern border, Vietnam was growing more powerful. Shortly after Mouhot's trip, the Cambodian monarchy would succumb to grinding French colonialism, becoming a French protectorate in order to combat its aggressive neighbors.

"Before crossing the lake it may, perhaps, be as well to say what remains to be told respecting the latter country," Mouhot wrote. "The present state of Cambodia is deplorable, and its future menacing."

On the Tonle Sap today, it feels that way once again.

Chang Laom has five children—none have stayed on the water. They've cast out across the country, settling in landlocked villages on small plots of soil. Those come with their own problems: drought and floods, failed crops and debt. Still, to them it seems far more viable than a life on the Tonle Sap.

"It's not easy to make a living from fishing. Some places are closed off. Some are lots for conservation. The police can arrest you and then you have to pay them," Laom explains. "It's difficult to live on the water."

The neighbors' kids, too, are following suit. She tells me how one or another left to work in construction, to work in a car wash, to work in Thailand. The same water that supported Laom for more than three decades is failing now.

Her children, poor as they are, keep urging their mother to come join them at their homes. She can't bring herself to leave though, not just yet.

I follow Laom back to her house, through her strange, scorched garden and on toward the riverbank. Behind us, the burnt earth is sharp against the blue skies. Laom folds herself into a low hammock, glancing at her husband who sits on the ground mending fishing nets.

At the shoreline, tall stalks of water grasses are packed tight between a clutch of floating houses. The water, visible only in a slice, mirrors back the green.

2 *Where There Is Water, There Are Fish*

A circle of water hyacinth floats in the middle of the sand-milk lake. It is huge, twenty feet in diameter, and growing. Young fishers, half a dozen friends, stand knee-deep in water and drag in plants. Two women use their boat as a giant's trowel, pushing it through a hyacinth patch, separating out yet more greenery to be pulled into their fishing circle. The plants are three feet tall, each spongy stalk topped with a massive jade heart of a leaf. They grow in clumps, roots a mud-clay tangle around their neighbors. The fishers sing while they work, joke, and as one group gathers the hyacinth, another slowly corrals the mass with a long span of net. It takes several hours to finish. When they're done, they've transformed the hyacinth into a green disc, tied up with netting, gently bobbing in place.

Then. Wait.

The sun is rising higher and the shallow lake grows warmer. Inside this makeshift forest, all is cool and shady. Soon, fish will start snaking their way in, drawn by the parasol leaves, the pleasant waters submerging the roots. For several hours, the temporary habitat will draw new residents by the hundreds. Until, at last, the time is right, and the fishing can begin.

Mending fishing nets is dry season work; how endless it can seem. One May morning, Chang Laom, her husband, Seng Kimluon, and their neighbors quietly work their way through yards of dull orange nets draped about them like wedding tulle. Their fingers seize on tears, jetting neon-green fishermen's needles through the worn mesh. Behind the menders, round net-and-bamboo fish traps are stacked by the dozen. Hunter-green nets spooled around three-foot poles lie piled against a tree.

So many nets for so few fish.

Kimluon has never seen as poor a catch as in 2016. "It's so different—there's probably 70 percent less fish this year."

There are clear reasons for the drop in fish, thinks Kimluon. "First, there's low water. It's completely dry here. Second is illegal fishing. They use equipment forbidden by the government inside the lake."

Kimluon's hair is brush thick and calicoed with black dye. A trim gray beard encircles a pensive mouth. He pauses his mending to talk; nearby, two neighbors girded against the sun in hats and fingerless gloves keep sharp eyes trained on the yards of netting piled between them.

Even this equipment has changed from when Kimluon first moved here in 1984. "It's a completely different business now. I used to use nets with big holes. Now, I have to use small hole nets since the fish are smaller and smaller."

In front of the menders, the river is low and turbid. Sharp crescents of morning glory leaves spread clover thick, dividing land from a row of barely floating houses. Plank walkways and blue-plastic piping cut past grounded boats and livestock pens. Kimluon's own house is on land, tilting on six-foot-tall stilts barely thicker than an arm. Bamboo poles gird the floorboards—come rainy season, they will be lashed to drums and set afloat.

Towering above us on twenty-foot poles stands a spirit house that is nearly as big as a real house and made of sturdier materials. Its walls are neat wood planking, its roof a slick zinc triangle. Here is where the community makes offerings to the guardian spirit of this land. Of late, it seems nothing will appease the *neak ta*.

In 1871 Lieutenant Jules Marcel Brossard de Corbigny, a French naval officer, set off from Phnom Penh toward Bangkok with a Cambodian mission to Siam. Traveling as part of a massive convoy that included eighty elephants, Brossard de Corbigny marveled at the abundance of the "Great Lake of miraculous fishing."[1]

"There, as early as January, everything is prepared for a productive harvest, vivified by freedom, free from all worries. A profit is secured for any fisherman, big or small," he wrote. As the water level began dropping, "the nets of three or four fishermen working together for the season connect end to end and form an immense seine capable of surrounding whole banks. The shivering on the surface indicates the presences of the fish. The bank's indication is soon surrounded by nets which gradually fall back on the compact mass of prisoners. They are then thrown by armfuls into the boats until they are filled, for it is by whole boats that the yield of a single scoop of the net is counted."

The lieutenant went on in this vein for several pages—detailing the profits and fees, the costs of boat and net repair, the negotiations between the French colonial government and Siam over how such fisheries ought to be taxed. (Within forty years, taxes from this abundant fishery would supply one-ninth of the French Protectorate's budget.)[2] His writing is breathless.

"In spite of this slaughter lasting nearly three months the lake is far from being depopulated. There is room for more farms . . . There could be more."

The sun is pushing through the clouds, beating down on the fishermen working a muddy channel downriver from Prek Toal. Four men stand in the water, which comes up to their waists, clearing muck from a net filled with thumb-sized fish. A man in a green bucket hat crouches inside a fiberglass boat and scoops at the netted fish with a shallow wicker basket. A fourteen-year-old boy sits in a second boat, giggling at his father's jokes.

At fifty-two, Suon Chhoeun is the elder of the group. His black hat is pulled low against the sun and the water has climbed up his shirt, soaking through, running clay patches across his chest.

He laughs when I lean out of our boat to ask how the fishing is, now, at the end of dry season in 2017.

"No, it's not a good business. It's just hand to mouth." Chhoeun pulls the net taut and his friends collect the last of the massing fish, depositing them into a small hamper resting in the teen's boat. The container is no bigger than the kid's encircled arms, and still it is barely half full, though the group has been at it for hours.

Chhoeun glances at the boy and predicts there won't be any fish left by the time he grows up.

"I was a fisherman since I was young. But now it's really a bad business, there aren't any fish," Chhoeun says. "I think the only way to fix it is to stop illegal fishing—stop fishing with electricity and so on. The big problem is in the middle of the Tonle Sap. Here, we're just doing family fishing."

His friend pipes up, annoyed: "They're not cracking down on the rich. Just on poor families."

Chhoeun thinks back to his boyhood, when he was five, six. "In the Lon Nol regime, fish would just jump into your boat." Big fish: Snakehead. Carp. Catfish. The men untangle the final few fish and heft themselves back into their boats to head home. Their net, pulled in and rinsed clean, now rests like a shroud in the bow—seemingly more useless by the day.

While the past few years have seen the worst catch yet, fishers' daily and yearly hauls have been dropping for decades. The available figures may be far from comprehensive, but they hint at the enormous transformation. In the 1940s the population of Cambodia comprised 3.2 million people, about a tenth of whom worked the lake.[3] Over the next half century, that lake dwelling population more than tripled. The overall catch pulled from the lake roughly doubled during that period—but the increase in population, coupled with the rise of commercial fisheries, meant each person was netting 44 percent less fish by the mid-1990s.[4]

The reasons for this are manifold. After a decade of civil war and the devastation wrought by the Khmer Rouge through the 1970s, the relative peace that followed brought with it a baby boom and skyrocketing economic growth. But that growth didn't translate into much opportunity for the poorest Cambodians. Fishing was viewed as a stable means of survival, something that could be done with scant investment. One of the intractable impacts of the Khmer Rouge era was the disarray in which it left Cambodia's land tenure. To this day, land disputes are a common occurrence. But for the longest time, striking a claim on the Tonle Sap remained relatively simple: all that was needed to live on the lake was the ability to hack away at a section of flooded forest in order to build a home. Those moving to floating villages needed even less: a boat and a tree to anchor on when the water rose.

Ahnah thebpahtai is a phrase Cambodians are fond of. Prime Minister Hun Sen peppers his speech with it, and my journalist friends love inserting it in their copy. It means "anarchy," and there is scarcely a better way to describe what happened to the lake after the fall of the Khmer Rouge. It became wildly popular to fish by throwing sticks of dynamite into the water, or by dipping in wires crackling with electricity from attached batteries—two ways to kill large numbers of fish quickly and easily. Big trawlers moved in. Overfishing became rampant.

Simultaneously, the diminishing forest exacted its own price. The Khmer Rouge decimated the jungles during its short reign, clearing an estimated thousand square miles of forest surrounding the lake.[5] Their efforts expanded on those of Cambodia's French colonialists, who—like the Angkorian kings long before them—tore the forest down for export, fuel, and to make room for crops that could be taxed.

That frenzy has continued unabated. In recent decades, the mantle has been taken up by powerful businessmen with ties to the highest reaches of government. Today Cambodia has among the highest rate of deforestation in the world, even within protected areas.[6] Rare, expensive timber is sold for a small fortune and the cleared land is then turned into rubber and palm oil plantations. The destruction is evident both nationally and on the Tonle Sap. Between the late 1960s and early 1990s, the forest surrounding the lake decreased in size by a third to just eleven hundred square miles—and shrinking—taking with it critical spawning and feeding grounds for the Tonle Sap's fish and sending soil spilling into the floodplains.[7]

Tucked in among the bejeweled kings and celestial apsaras, among the vivid scenes of Cham naval battles and Hindu epics and daily court life, hundreds of fish swim across the sandstone walls of Angkor Wat and Bayon.[8]

Fish float above a group of men gathering for a cockfight and edge past a vendor. A man balances on a delicate boat as he casts his net into a throng of giant fish. A woman entices customers to buy a fish the size of a child. There are dead fish: poisoned by the churning of the sea of milk. There are carp, there are eels, there is a mythical fish with the nose of an elephant. Abducted by a demon and thrown into the ocean, Pradyumna, eldest son of Lord Vishnu, sits calmly inside a fish. A large fish swallows a small goat. A school of fish passes through a tangle of lotus roots. As a battle roars across the surface of the lake, fish gently thread their way between the sailors' oars.

Scattered across the temples, these bas-reliefs advertise the outsized importance and the omnipresence of fish in Angkorian life. "There are very many fish whose names I don't know, all of them coming from the Freshwater Sea," wrote Zhou Daguan, the Chinese emissary sent to the Angkorian kingdom at the end of the thirteenth century.

"There are giant soft-shell turtles and alligators as big as large pillars . . . there are crocodiles as big as boats," he wrote upon his return to China. Is it any surprise the lake's prodigious fishery drew such delight from Zhou? "They get clams, mud clams and pond snails just by scooping them out of the Freshwater Sea."

On April 17, 1975, after years of slowly gaining territory, the Khmer Rouge won control of Phnom Penh and began installing one of the most barbaric governments in modern history. The entire population of Phnom Penh was marched out of their homes and dispersed across the countryside. Elsewhere, including in many of the villages surrounding the lake, occupation by the Khmer Rouge came even earlier—here, too, people were moved from their homes and assigned to worksites. Fishers became rice farmers and laborers—slaves, really—like everyone else. The family unit was destroyed. A civilian's only allegiance was expected to be to the Khmer Rouge, at the cost of death for those who defied their orders.

Democratic Kampuchea operated as an internment camp the size of a nation, with its citizens laboring from dawn to dusk on the scantiest of food rations. Much of the country was employed in ill-organized collective farming schemes, while the rest worked on infrastructure projects like dams and irrigation canals. The country was closed off to the outside world, in a lunatic bid at self-reliance (inspired, ever so loosely, by the fallen grandeur of Angkor).

Upending a functioning system of agriculture and closing off trade had disastrous consequences. By the time the Vietnamese seized Phnom Penh on January 7, 1979, toppling the regime, an estimated 2.2 million Cambodians had either been killed by Khmer Rouge cadres or had died of starvation, overwork, and preventable diseases. A quarter of the population was lost. The severing of communities, institutional destruction, and sweeping trauma would shape the country for decades to come.

The Khmer Rouge, of course, did not rise to power in a vacuum. In the preceding years, a so-called secret bombing campaign by the U.S. government ravaged a neutral Cambodia. Secret to whom? Certainly not those suffering the impact. Even today, craters litter Cambodia's countryside, the imprint of bombs showered down by B52s.[9] Aiming to cut off North Vietnamese supply lines, the U.S. dropped hundreds of thousands of tons of explosives on Cambodia (the remnants of which continue to kill and maim to this day). Tens of thousands of Cambodians were killed, villages were destroyed, and the agriculture-based economy collapsed. As the political and economic turmoil worsened, Prime Minister Norodom Sihanouk—the volatile, charming, and beloved king who abdicated the throne to enter politics—was overthrown in a 1970 coup.

Sihanouk was replaced by a corrupt, U.S.-backed general named Lon Nol, and the country rapidly devolved even further. Farmers fled the bombings, the economy continued to plunge, and Sihanouk—fatefully— aligned himself with the Khmer Rouge, giving the guerrillas far wider support. Civil war between the Khmer Rouge and Lon Nol's government gained strength, sending ever more hungry, impoverished, and traumatized refugees surging into Phnom Penh. As the Khmer Rouge moved closer to the city, the U.S. cut off military aid and foreign embassies began evacuating. When the regime finally took the capital in 1975, many celebrated, if only for a moment. After eight years of civil war, this, they believed, represented the end to violence, fear, and hunger.

Between the bombings, the civil war, and the Khmer Rouge, Cambodians faced a decade of horror. The years that followed, which included Vietnamese occupation, continued Western and Chinese support for the Khmer Rouge, and ongoing guerrilla warfare were hardly a return to normalcy. But people pushed forward with their lives. After the Khmer Rouge fell in 1979, countless Cambodians fled across the Thai border, joining the largest refugee camps in the world at the time. Millions more remade their lives within the country—returning to their home villages, taking over spaces inhabited only by ghosts.

Others settled into new areas entirely. The Tonle Sap, with its seemingly limitless food supply, made for an appealing home.

Horm Sok was part of that wave of new lake dwellers—survivors seeking out a life that could be sustained by a widely available natural resource. After the Khmer Rouge fell and the population could move more freely, Sok followed his adopted father to a floating village.

For many living on the Tonle Sap, the years that followed are remembered as a time of relative abundance. "During the Khmer Rouge, no one caught any fish—so after, there were a lot. Once I spent three days collecting fish from just one net," Sok recounts when we speak in 2017.

As a teenager, Sok and his father caught fish as part of a community group. In the early 1980s these lighter forms of collectivization briefly gained traction under the Vietnamese-backed government as a way to stoke economic development.[10] In Sok's group, local officials provided nets and basic equipment. The work, and the catch, was divided equally among the members.

"At that time, fish were everywhere. We'd drive the boat and fish would jump in."

Today, Sok lives in Akol, a small floating village on the southern edge of the lake. He's still a fisherman, but for the past decade he has also worked as a field researcher—hired by a conservation group to collect data on fish hauls. Four times each month, Sok sets out a thirty-yard net and records the catch: the amount, weight, and species. The end of dry season has always seen lower yields, but rarely this low, Sok says.

"I started measuring in 2012. Then, one net would yield about three kilos. Now it's one kilo or a half kilo per net. I think it's because fishers are using many types of illegal methods."

Sok pauses to clarify: it's big fishing operations using these methods. Those living in communities like his can barely get by. It's hard to imagine anything they do to catch fish might be cutting into the dwindling supply.

"The people who live here have seen that since they were born there is no improvement. They just live hand to mouth. If they get a bit of money, they have to use it to fix their house, to buy vegetables, to fix their boat. I have been here more than thirty years and it seems nothing has improved."

All around him, Sok sees people desperate to leave this lake.

"If they could save some money, they could move to land. Now, people really want to do that—but land is so expensive."

Life on the Tonle Sap has never been easy, but it was survivable for so long. That hardly seems the case anymore. There's a question Sok thinks about often these days: "How can we get as much fish as before?"

The fish smoker is an old man, hair shorn tight along his temples. He stokes his fire as the sun sets, blue clouds billowing past a group of children playing in the road. His smoker is a loose, low brick box, perhaps fifteen feet long and no taller than his waist, flames glowing through its chinks. On top sits a grill made of mesh covered with thousands of finger-length fish. Over several hours, they will slowly cure, skin pulling tight against desiccated flesh, until transformed into a food stable enough to be hawked for hours on a hot city street. They look like raked leaves now, piles of fine brown and white flake. The man carefully makes his way along the length of his smoker, section by section, lifting the grill, agitating the fish with a stick, turning and turning as the sweet-smelling smoke rises above. Behind him, the sun has almost dropped below the inlet and a neighbor cooks her dinner on an outdoor stove—her small flames bright against the rising dark.

For as long as humans have lived near the Tonle Sap, its fisheries have played a crucial role in feeding and growing communities.

Centuries before Angkorian artisans chiseled fat snakeheads and giant carp onto the powerful kings' temples, people living near the lake feasted on Tonle Sap fish.

Ancient lakeside burial mounds hold the entombed remains of cooked meals: fish salted and marinated; fish turned into soup; fish roasted and smoked. Excavations of Bronze Age archaeological sites feature numerous species of captured fish—some that twist into Cambodian nets to this day, others that are nearly extinct.

In 2004 there was a significant drought, awful for fishers, but an unusual boon for researchers. As water receded across the Western Baray—a mammoth six-square-mile hand-cut Angkorian reservoir—the nearly four-thousand-year-old necropolis of Koh Ta Meas became accessible.[11] Zooarchaeologist Voeun Vuthy and his team meticulously collected some ten thousand fragments of animal bones—buffalo and pigs, deer and chickens and cattle, tigers and elephants. And, of course, fish.

When they analyzed the fish fragments they discovered sixteen distinct families. Half came from the Tonle Sap Lake, including, astonishingly, the Irrawaddy dolphin—which is now nearly extinct from the entirety of the Mekong and had never previously been recorded in the lake.

At a nearby fifteen-hundred-year-old archaeological site called Prei Khmeng, the team uncovered and analyzed hundreds more fish bones. These fish were so big they would have required special equipment to catch them, Vuthy deduced. Thousands of years before the great builders of Angkor carved the hydrological city from the banks of the Tonle Sap, fishers here were using a unique set of skills to exploit the lake's vast fishery. The shallow lake was full of monsters; so abundant, it must have been impossible to imagine they could ever disappear.

Mekong giant catfish can reach 650 pounds and spawn after migrating from Vietnam all the way to Cambodia, Laos, and Thailand. They look like their diminutive namesake only as much as a dinosaur resembles a lizard. As the Mekong's fisheries dwindle, the biggest blow is to the immense diversity of species, the legion of midsize fish that made up ordinary, daily catch. But the disappearance of megafauna like *Pangasianodon gigas* stings differently: an epic loss, an irreplaceable one.

Most fishers have never seen one of these critically endangered fish; fewer still have netted one. If they did, it was almost certainly a long time ago. "I caught one before Pol Pot's time, never since," a seventy-five-year-old fisherman named Preap Chea says. He's sitting inside a small ticket office alongside a Siem Reap inlet at the northern tip of the lake, where the rare tourist can spend $3 for entry into a nearby floating village. Tacked up behind Chea's desk are cheery posters featuring scores of native fish species: an inadvertent who's-who of what's become endangered.

"Now there's not a lot of fish because some of our people don't respect the law on illegal fishing," he says, with a shake of his head. As for Mekong giant catfish, "We really don't see this type of fish anymore. Last year, I saw some fishermen catch one, but they released it."

Any fisher who managed to catch a giant catfish will remember it. His eyes light up. It's a marvel, a once-in-a-lifetime event.

So the old fish tales go like this: In 1992 Yem Yun caught a two-hundred-pound giant catfish. How big was it? So big, his boat nearly collapsed. So big, no one dared to buy it so, instead, "we just cut it up and dried it. It lasted three or five days and we shared it with all our relatives and neighbors."

Twenty-five years—that's how long it's been since Yun spotted one of these monsters. "If I saw one now, I wouldn't catch it," he says, somberly. "If you see it, you must let it get away."

3 *Don't Let a Hungry Man Guard Rice*

The fishermen come at night. They come just before dawn. They come alone and they come in pairs. They push out from shredding homes on the edge of the Tonle Sap and head in-water as quietly as possible. They cut across one conservation zone marker, then another, land fading to a smudge.

Beneath the bruised wood hulls, the water shifts. No longer brackish and still, dishwater dull, set through with oil and soap and the touch of so many people. Here, the lake is spackled silver. And it heaves with fish.

Pick a night in early 2016—the drought has been dragging on and on and the catch has dwindled to nearly nothing. There's no money, and there's too much debt, and no one's getting near enough to eat. When the fishermen cast here, though, their nets swell like some miracle. Gills spark light from the moon. The only sounds come from fat bodies slapping the gunwales, motors beelike in the distance.

Here is the thing about fishing in the conservation zone: it's wrong, but there are trawlers out there every night and there's plenty of guys with more money than anyone here will see in a lifetime slipping it to police. Even as the Tonle Sap dries up, big fish are still somehow being pulled by the tons from deep inside the lake. What harm can one small fisherman cause?

This is what Sok Keo thinks as he glides out there in his tiny boat. It's a simple calculation—mouths to feed and this, seemingly, the only spot in the whole lake with fish. Of course conservation is important; Keo is a fisherman, no fool, and has seen how the catch has plummeted since he was a kid. But a lone man, fishing only for himself and his family, how can this be wrong? It seems unfathomable that their survival is against the law. He casts as discreetly as possible, but when the authorities arrive to stop him, it is barely a surprise.

The operations center for the Krakor District Fisheries patrol is a large blue houseboat anchored a few miles out from the lake's southwestern edge. Smaller boats ring its edge—there's a dilapidated wood rowboat and standard fiberglass longboards sporting souped-up engines. There's a speedboat too, garish against these ordinary vessels, rust weeping across its slick frame. Still more boats sit wedged against hundreds of yards of old fishing net lying on a nearby wooden platform. The nets drip over the pier's edge, snaking down the stilts, dipping into water that even here is barely thigh-high in May 2016.

Inside, the boat serves as a station, dorm, and dining room. Batteries and walkie-talkies sit in a nest of wires underneath a desk messy with papers. Across the room, plastic jugs of drinking water line the wall. A shelf runs half the length of the boat, packed with flowery bedrolls and toiletries: buckets of soap, toothpaste, and combs packed haphazardly among the sheets. On one wall, a chart featuring local fish species peeks out from behind a shrine. A broad, wood deck encircles the houseboat. Here, a sad sight: a small monkey tied to a tire rim by a short length of chain. Entertainment for long, dull days in what sometimes seems like the middle of nowhere.

The waters of the Tonle Sap on this drought day strike a strange chord. The lake is so low and so rimmed with copper-colored algae that it looks like a sandy desert floor. Red streaks out toward the land, toward hills fading shadow-blue against the sky. When fishers are caught in the conservation zone, this is where they are brought.

Pen Vuthy, the Krakor district fisheries' chief, instructs his men to show us some of the illegal equipment they've confiscated in recent days. In they come, dragging a plastic barrel shorn in half and filled with netting, upending it on the floor. The fishing net is made of soft white stuff, tied to two slender bits of wood with knots and bark still visible. A baby's hand could fit through these holes. I hadn't seen such large and simple netting during any of my trips and it was hard to imagine much could be caught with that.

"This is legal equipment, but they're using it in the wrong place," Vuthy explains.

Vuthy has been working in this area in some form or another since the 1980s. He has little of the swagger or bluster of most "authorities." No gold watch on his wrist, no rings whatsoever. No beer belly, even. While the other officers strain the buttons of their khaki shirts, Vuthy's hangs loose against his tall frame. He speaks in a tone of genuine sympathy about the illegal fishers he and his twenty-two men have been catching of late.

"It's not the big criminals now," he says. The drought has "really impacted the people living in this area. When they can't fish it really affects their life. They can't have enough to support their families. Before, they'd catch about fifty kilos a day, this year it's not even five."

The area that falls under Vuthy's control is about ten square miles. Inside this portion of lake, fish fry are meant to grow unmolested— given a chance to thrive before migrating out toward the Tonle Sap and Mekong Rivers. The closer a fisher gets to the edges of this conservation zone, the greater his chance of a decent catch. Deep inside, of course, is where the best fishing lies.

For desperate fishers, the conservation zone has proven impossible to resist. Even if it's rainy or windy, "they take the boat and cover it in plastic. They tie it to a post and try to be quiet," says Vuthy.

He and his men set off at dusk and don't return until after 8 a.m. most mornings. They copy tactics from the fishers themselves—snorkels underwater, driving with the lights off. With the drought raging on, it's hard to keep up.

"More and more crime is happening. It's like if there's a beautiful daughter in your home—the men want to come inside. Outside, they can't fish, so they run the risk by coming in the protected area, even if they face jail."

In truth, Vuthy's "little criminals" are rarely sent to jail—though their punishment is hardly more compassionate. Those caught during the nightly patrols are brought to the houseboat and made to sign a paper promising not to return. Their equipment—the whole of their livelihood—may be confiscated. A fine is often meted out.

"Some of them beg me to release their nets to them, but I can't do it. I need to report it to the commune chief and district chief. I make them sign a paper saying they won't come back. Mostly they respect it—we educate them and they don't come back. The fishermen don't think about the future of the fish. They just think about today."

In March 2017, a year after being caught fishing in the conservation zone, Sok Keo is still paying back his fine. At forty-seven, he is already a widower. His eldest son is twenty-five, but most of his five children are school-age. Children need to eat and 2016 was a bad year for it.

Keo lives in Kampong Prek, a small floating village located perhaps twenty minutes by boat from Vuthy's outpost and the edge of the conservation zone. Just a few dozen families moor here, hugging a sparse flooded forest and following the shoreline inland when the water level rises. While big floating villages boast health centers and schools, mechanics and churches, Kampong Prek is among the sparest sort. One house has an awning made from brightly colored cardboard beer cases. Torn tarps serve as temporary walls and roofs and billow at a breeze. The floats beneath the houses come in the form of long stalks of bamboo lashed together, or else rusting steel oil drums.

We pull our boat up close to Keo's to talk. Dressed in a white button-up shirt, his graying hair clipped close around his ears, Keo could pass for an office worker, from a distance. He sits tall in the center of one of the small, turquoise wooden boats that are ubiquitous in these waterways.

At the height of the drought, Keo set out for the nearest conservation area and cast his nets. "There was a huge shortage of fish, and I didn't know what else to do," he says. He was caught almost immediately and ordered to purchase 150 liters of gasoline for the patrols—a fine equal to about $130. The figure is so impossibly high, Keo has had to peel money off from a microfinance loan meant for fishing equipment and boat repair.

"Other people here have been arrested by fisheries officials. But we have no fish, so we have to go there," says Keo.

While Keo speaks, his two youngest children look on. They are barefoot, wearing dirty pants and weary expressions. His ten-year-old daughter straddles the prow, toes skimming the water. Her older brother jumps out and begins wading toward their house. All three have been out fishing today, pulling in their sherbet-orange traps to gather a respectable twenty pounds of small gray shrimp. After a very bad year, that rates as a decent catch.

"We used to be able to fish around here, but now most of it is the conservation zone. I think it's good for the fish," Keo offers. "But I think for small scale fishing they should still allow us to fish there. It's such a big size and there's so much fish."

After leaving Keo we turn our boat away from the shore and chug farther into the lake, heading toward the fisheries patrol station. I want to see if I can find an official who remembers Keo and who could explain what he had been caught with and why his fine would have been so steep. Vuthy isn't there and the uniformed men we find don't want to speak with us. But as we push into the deeper waters of the conservation area, I watch in awe as the surface of the lake begins to pulse. Fish, the length of my forearm, twist from the water, spasming above the surface and landing with a thud. Did I shout or stand in silence, watching those thrashing fish? In my entire time on the lake, this is the only firsthand glimpse I'd get of what had been lost.

"Fishermen catch fish," the shop owner, Heng, had pointed out on an earlier trip. "If they can't, what happens?"

Much later, I'd wonder how anyone whose existence was predicated on this sole action could possibly resist such a place.

There were fish "the size of the sperm whale," Lieutenant Brossard de Corbigny observed in wonder in 1871.[1] When the water level dropped, boats heavy with fish were "hauled from bank to bank by several pairs of buffaloes to reach the distant villages." When the lake was at its highest, anyone living at its edges simply walked to the water each morning and descended "into the stream with a piece of net, his basket, or his bowl, with some sort of container in a word, and beating the water with a lot of yelling and frolicking . . ." soon had "caught myriads of frightened fish, which provide for the requirements of the kitchen."

At the border of Battambang, barely ten miles from where the French lieutenant stopped to marvel at the fisheries of Siem Reap, slender, grass-lined rivers snake from the lake toward the protected wetlands of Prek Toal.

These waterways cut through verdant patches of mangroves and snowy egrets glide low. All along those channels lie hundreds of fish traps—nets spooled around stakes driven into the soft river floor. Such traps are often deemed illegal: made with wood cut from the protected area, for instance, or with nets featuring holes smaller than what is permitted by the fisheries law.

"When we install the traps, the fish officials come and take them," says Mok Nhor.

"Six days ago, the fishery officials came and took our traps. They say they are illegal," his wife, Sok Chetra, adds. "But if we can't do this, we will die."

The couple, now in their late seventies, have lived in one spot or another along the Tonle Sap's northern tip since they were teenagers. In early 2017, they are occupying a slender span of auburn riverbank. Both are bald, heads neatly shaved. On Nhor's biceps, the faded remains of a traditional tattoo peek through. He squats, his back curved like a delicate crescent, offering a polite, befuddled smile. His wife, just one year younger, hums with energy.

Over the course of Nhor and Chetra's adulthood, life on the Tonle Sap has changed unaccountably.

"Before we didn't really use money, we exchanged fish or *prahok* for rice," Chetra recounts wistfully. Her husband is hard of hearing, so she speaks for both, strong hands pulsing in the air as she talks.

"A long time ago fish jumped into the boat, now not even trey kampleanh jump in," she says, referring to a type of gourami, about the size of a hand.

I ask them what types of fish have disappeared—Chetra thinks a moment, then ticks them off, one by one.

"Trey khmann, trey krai, trey krawlang," she tells us: a footlong cyprinid, a long, thin knifefish, a hefty mud carp.[2] "There's no trey reach now." She hasn't seen a single giant catfish in thirty-two years. "We used to see them here, now there are none."

Cambodia is a country of young people. Two-thirds of the population is under the age of thirty, less than a tenth older than sixty, and just a slim fraction above seventy-five.[3] Chetra and Nhor would have been children when Cambodia gained independence from France and well into adulthood when the Khmer Rouge took power. All eight of their children died during the Khmer Rouge; they never had another.

For many years, the couple lived in a floating home. Once that became damaged beyond repair, they moved to this slip of land. Their house is a sort of temporary shelter made of a thin wood platform balanced on bamboo stakes. In place of walls, there is plastic sheeting and palm thatching. This ground is available mostly because of its sheer inhabitability. After the rains start, the swelling lake eventually engulfs this strip of land and the couple moves to a nearby pagoda—sleeping on its hard cement floors night after night until the time has come to pack up and return to the riverbank. Their life is compressed to bare survival. And so, to this couple, the actions of the fisheries patrols seem beyond overzealous; they tilt toward outright cruelty.

As Chetra speaks, a boat stuffed with officers jets by and she pauses to watch them pass. They're driving through, she thinks, to pull up the rows of traps dotting the river.

"They come every five or six days," Chetra says, tired of this game. "It's like this: we give money to you and you don't confiscate the nets," she says, peering in my direction, "but then you come instead," she looks at my colleague.

In the end, the authorities get the nets and the money. The fishers are left with nothing.

Until a decade ago, large portions of the Tonle Sap were divided into fishing lots. Buyers bid as much as several hundred thousand dollars for a two-year license that gave them exclusive rights to all fish inside their lot—an area that could span hundreds of square miles.[4] Countless trees were sacrificed to the lots, which were bordered with posts and massive bamboo blankets that trapped fish inside during the growing season. This system had existed in some form or another since Angkorian times. At its modern peak, in the 1990s and 2000s, the lots were considered among the most complex and developed fisheries regulatory systems in the world.[5]

What did this remarkable system look like? Anarchy. Private militias patrolled the fishing lot boundaries, arresting, fining, and occasionally killing intruders. Trespassing was common because at their height, less than twenty individually owned lots covered 80 percent of the lake. While that allotted portion included much of the lake's prime fishing territory, individual fishers could, possibly, have supported themselves on what remained. But lot owners routinely expanded their boundaries: pushing border poles farther and farther out into public fishing areas and bribing officers to look the other way.[6]

The system was deeply mismanaged and abused, and every so often Cambodia's long-serving strongman prime minister, Hun Sen, would cancel certain lots as part of a populist bid. Finally, in the lead-up to what would prove a particularly contentious election, Hun Sen in early 2012 annulled the fishing lot system entirely. Across the lake, at least thirty-five remaining lots then totaling an estimated 230 square miles were released.[7] One-third of the area was set aside for conservation purposes, with the rest to be managed by community fishery associations.

While fishers and some researchers initially celebrated the end of the fishing lots, the intervening years have been disheartening. Lots that were transformed into conservation zones proved open to the same corruption that ruined the original system. Those that became community fisheries have been difficult to protect against overfishing. Illegal fishing has become stubbornly entrenched. As individual hauls diminish, small scale fishers increasingly have to rely on illicit means: fishing in protected areas or using banned tools such as nets made of very fine mesh. In 2018 alone, fisheries officials collected nearly 1.5 million yards of illegal fishing nets and hundreds of illegal traps.[8]

But it is the large-scale operations, carried out through bribery and collusion, that are destroying fish stocks. Groups of fishermen working on behalf of wealthy sellers use massive nets strung between boats and large-scale electrocution to catch fish by the ton. Community groups have reported that nightly bribes for such illegal activity can reach thousands of dollars.[9] "Last year there were so many trawlers, if you looked at the lake it was dark," a fisherman told me in 2017.

The government occasionally acknowledges the extent of the problem. In late 2016 Prime Minister Hun Sen created a task force to combat illegal fishing on the lake. But while the four-month campaign saw the release of twenty-two tons of live fish, only thirty-six people were arrested and authorities never disclosed what charges or convictions ensued.[10] Were those arrested the businessmen who own the boats? The fishermen working the big nets? The police taking bribes? Perhaps they were three dozen family fishers like Sok Keo.

The sprawling floating village of Kampong Luong sits on the southern rim of the Tonle Sap, a few miles from Kampong Prek and from the fisheries patrol boat. To the tiny floating villages skirting this edge of the lake, Kampong Luong is like the big city—with its shops and mechanics and schools. Hundreds of families live at this relatively choice spot just past where the dirt road leading from Krakor town spills into the lake.

It's early morning, the sun just beginning to burn off the dawn chill, and Lem Sita is already up and dressed. Her turtleneck pokes out above a pajama suit covered with impressionistic red and yellow flowers; her graying hair is pulled tightly back. Breakfast is noodle soup, purchased from a passing vendor, the steam fogging her glasses with each bite.

Sita is a fish buyer and her home, which doubles as the center of her business operations, is anchored at the edge of Kampong Luong.

It's a fine old houseboat, broad and sturdy like a little ship. Its wood flooring is so meticulously clean it's hard to believe that thousands of pounds of fish cross its surface each day. Empty orange coolers, the size of small trucks, line one side of the boat. Hammocks for the workers are tucked neatly into the boat's rafters. Sita sits in a plastic chair on the open deck. Behind her, an accordion gate, key still hanging from lock, has been pulled open to reveal the boat's innards. On the front of a broad metal desk, she's taped a cheery cardboard *Fú*, the Chinese character for good luck, set between a pair of carp. Opposite the desk sits a small house shrine with a needlepoint tablet. A calendar on the wall has already been flipped to today's date, May 26, 2016. Boxes of bottled water are stacked in one corner. Farther back lies the kitchen, its dishes parked in tidy rows.

Before the fishing lots were closed, Sita ran one—a family business going back generations. If the poorest members of the public suffered from the fishing lot set up, the owners thrived. It was in the owners' interest (as attested to by their militias) to regulate catch inside their lots, allowing the fish to grow. Now, there's far less fish, and what comes in is much smaller.

"It's quite different this year. There's not enough water, and there's no fish. As you can see, it's very low water, so people can't fish." She looks out over the stretch of water leading into the lake. The water is always dirty here: such a big village, so many people. But this is worse. It's chocolate-brown today, covered with a seeping oil slick and a fine layer of copper algae. When a motorboat cuts through the water, churning the algae, it turns pea-green in the wake. Nothing looks as it should.

"I just want to know, if the water is this low—can they save it?"

The conservation zone is talked about constantly on the lake. Every fisher, it seems, has an opinion on these porous enclosures set aside by "the authorities." (Every official, too, of course, has his own take on the matter.) In a country plagued by the dual ills of corruption among the most powerful and desperation among the least, the protected areas prove a ripe meeting ground for these two forces.

Local activists report rampant graft. "They use large trawlers to catch the fish. Those fishermen earn $1,000 and pay $200 as a bribe," says An Socheat, a community leader from Prek Toal. "Across all six provinces along the Tonle Sap, there are many types of officials who come and take money."

Another activist meets us in a cafe in Battambang and walks us through the situation. "Rich people use thousand- or two-thousand-meter-long nets—how could they do that without the authorities' collusion?" he points out. But if the large and midsize fishing expeditions in conservation areas are decimating fisheries, he argues that even at the small scale, illicit fishing adds up. This is particularly visible among the protected wetlands encircling the lake.

"There's illegal activity in the flooded forest—they cut it for fishing, for traps, for farming. If 10 percent of people are doing this activity, well there's two or three million people in this area. According to the law, if you live there, you can't do anything—you can't fish or use the forest. But you go to that area and there are one hundred families, how could they survive if they're not fishing? They cut the forest for their fish traps, fish, and pay the officials half of what they make."

Consternation crosses his face as he contemplates what it would take to stop such behavior.

"It's impossible," he says, finally. "We have to set up some sort of association to give them other jobs. They cannot just rely on the fish."

The activist doesn't want his name to be used; his work is too sensitive. Environmentalists, rights workers, journalists, unionists—each year, a handful of critics, sometimes more, are arrested for their efforts. Occasionally they are hurt. Sometimes they're killed. The activist has been working closely with the fishing communities, teaching them how to collect evidence of large-scale illegal fishing and how to come together as a group to confront and halt the culprits. These types of patrols have gained traction in Cambodia's forests, and some have made an impact in stemming deforestation. On the lake, though, it's never quite worked.

"You look at people on the lake, from Angkorian time to almost today there's not much difference," the activist says. Now, however, climate change, dams, overpopulation, illegal fishing: all of it is swirling around these communities. "Before, we ate very big fish. For another five to ten years from now we'll still have the ability to fish. But beyond that, they will have to find another way—migration or another job."

The water, lower than anyone recalls seeing before, means the fish aren't moving or breeding as usual. Most years, Sita buys and sells several tons of fish each day. In 2016 that figure is down to a daily average of perhaps two hundred pounds.

"I don't know about the future situation, I just know this year the water is so low. There are so many problems, the people who live in the lake can't fish."

Sita's five children all moved out long ago and started different businesses in Battambang, on land. She hopes to be able to follow them soon enough. After generations, this family enterprise has come to an end. "My parents worked as fish sellers, now it's just me, I'm the last one—my kids don't want to do it, it's very tiring," she says. "If you live on land, at least you can grow rice."

A woman rows up to Sita on a tiny boat and passes her a little bag of whitefish in exchange for about $0.75. Another comes by offering a dollar's worth for sale. The fish seller, accustomed to dealing in the tons, will take what she can get.

"There's really no more business for fish buying," says Sita. There are the conservation areas, regulations around nets, rules on which months fishing is allowed; so very many laws.

"If you stay here permanently, you can't make a living from fishing year-round. If you try, you'll be arrested." She sympathizes with those who try and sneak their way into conservation zones. "All fishermen want to go to wherever there is fish."

4 *Navigate a River by Following Its Bends*

It's a March afternoon in Kampong Khleang and the boats keep coming down the muddy river leading from the Tonle Sap, docking to unload their haul, stilt houses casting shadows up the bank. The boats are battered square boxes, long and low, filled halfway up to the gunwales with watery masses of fish. Skinny teenagers in broad hats and flip-flops balance on the thwarts to shovel the catch into plastic baskets. When each basket is full, a pair of men slide it down the plank leading to the bank and drag it by its rope handles twenty yards up. Kids lie in wait with small nets, ready to snag any escapees.

The village sits about thirty miles southeast of Siem Reap city and the temples of Angkor, a mass of towering homes packed against one another along the lake's northern rim. Each day, thousands of pounds of fish will pass through this one small market alone. Countless more will go through countless markets set along countless inlets across the Tonle Sap. And at this particular spot on this particular day in 2017, there is only one type of fish the buyers are interested in: *trey riel*, which flicker like silver coins when the nets are drawn up.

The largest freshwater family in the world is *Cyprinidae*, among them carps and minnows, silvery and delicate. *Trey riel*—money fish—is the Khmer name for several of its species. Most are no larger than a thumb, though some can grow to the size of a forearm. Riel is the country's currency, but think of this fish like a 100 riel note—about $0.02—something even the poor have plenty of. Trey riel is oily and astoundingly nutritious. It is used, most commonly, in the fermented fish paste *prahok*—a staple so omnipresent only rice is more commonly seen on a Cambodian table. It is not hyperbole to say that in all of Cambodia, no animal is as important as trey riel.

Past the trey riel buyers, farther up the bank, the prahok makers are already at work. Two of the plastic baskets have ended up here, under the shade of a house. This is how prahok is made: rinse the fish, chop off the head, gut, and slake off the fingernail scales. Do this with a cleaver on a small wooden board, do this squatting, do this in several movements so swift they're hard to catch. This is a small-scale operation, the women and their daughters hired at a few dollars a day. But the basics apply equally to the industrial processor or the home cook. Leave the cleaned fish in fresh water overnight. Mix the fish with piles of salt, spread them out to dry for several days, pound them by hand or by machine, add spices and transfer the mixture to a jar or a bucket, a ceramic basin, a giant metal tub. And then: wait. When it has fermented adequately—for twenty days or several months or more than a year—the prahok is ready to eat.

Some forms are mild, but most are pungent and sharp, the scent of precisely what it is: fermented fish. Eat prahok with rice, at home, or dip icy sliced vegetables into it at the beer garden. Get the type that comes in blocks and fry it. Drop a spoonful of the watery version into the stew, the frying meat, the steaming greens. Cambodians eat, on average, 140 pounds of fish each year (44 pounds is the global average).[1] Don't underestimate how large a portion of that comes from prahok—about half of the Tonle Sap catch is trey riel. In Laos, the fish is fermented into *padaek*; in Thailand it's called *pla ra*. Any cyprinids that escape this fate are still consumed by the ton: salted and dried, smoked, roasted between splits of bamboo, thrown into soup.

The women in Kampong Khleang are working late in the year; the large-scale prahok industry operates in a brief season, from December to February when the cyprinids surge out of the lake toward the Mekong. Along the Tonle Sap River, *dais*—massive five-hundred-foot-long bag nets slung behind stationary boats and platforms—form a series of Vs leading up to the mouth of the lake. Around 150 years old, these seasonal dai fisheries were introduced to the Tonle Sap by Vietnamese fishers and formalized by the French. They have operated in more or less the same manner since their inception: Workers swing in the dais, spill their contents into waiting boats, and release the nets out once more. At the height of the season, six tons of trey riel can be collected in this manner each hour.

And even still, the dais are catching just a fraction. Of migrating fish, there is none more abundant than the cyprinids. When they surge, they are hunting for new habitats, for cool, dark places to survive as the Great Lake shrinks inward, stealing their homes. Trey riel will travel a dozen miles each day, hundreds of miles across the Mekong basin—to Laos, and even Thailand. They eddy up the Mekong into its tributaries, reaching fishers in every corner of the basin.[2]

Only now, the route they have followed for eons is gradually being sealed off.

The Mekong River wends some twenty-seven hundred miles from its source at the mountain-ringed Tibetan plateau to its mouth, where Vietnam's delta spills into the South China Sea. Nearly half of the river lies in China, where it is called the Lancang. From there, the Mekong traces the Golden Triangle linking Myanmar, Thailand, and Laos before meandering along the border of Thailand and Laos, flowing into Cambodia, and arcing toward Vietnam. Along the way, this river feeds into numerous tributaries both large and small, spanning a three-hundred-thousand-square-mile river basin that provides fish, fresh water, nutrients, and irrigation to millions of people.

The lower Mekong basin, which starts near the Laos-China border, is a broad mass of tributaries covering most of Laos and Cambodia and significant parts of Thailand and Vietnam. At its widest, the basin nearly reaches Bangkok in the west and the Gulf of Tonkin in the east. In all, three-quarters of the Mekong basin lies south of China, and even more of its water does—about 85 percent of the volume that flows out of the river comes from the lower Mekong basin.[3] While Southeast Asia's lower basin is a bulging spread of rivers and wetlands, China's upper basin is long and thin. The Lancang feeds few tributaries in China. Instead, it rushes through steep, narrow canyons—an ideal landscape for hydropower damming.

Since the 1990s China has gone on a dam-building spree. Eleven dams are now operational on the mainstem of the Lancang, a twelfth is under construction, and a thirteenth is planned.[4] The dams impact fish migration and block many tons of silt from flowing downstream—necessary for moving soil nutrients, preventing erosion, and keeping saltwater from the delta. Perhaps most crucially, the Lancang dams have reservoirs capable of holding trillions of gallons of water—something that is changing the lower Mekong basin in staggering ways.[5]

In recent years, the impact of those upstream dams has come into sharp focus. While the Lancang typically contributes just a small portion of downstream water flow, about 15 percent, the figure rises steeply during the dry season, and even more so in a drought—when as much as half of the lower Mekong's water comes from China. Possessing full control of the taps, Beijing now holds outsized power. In 2019, while Laos, Thailand, Cambodia, and Vietnam suffered from the worst drought in a century, China held back an unprecedented amount of water—effectively starving its downstream neighbors of their river. China insisted they discharged sufficient water and suffered their own low rainfall. But satellite images showed an amply wet China, in possession of more than enough water to spare. Had the flow not been restricted, in fact, the lower Mekong basin would have experienced an ordinary dry season—not a drought.[6]

The Lancang dams have an enormous impact but are hardly the only ones reshaping the lower Mekong basin. Laos has several mainstem dams operational, with plans for more, and Cambodia has explored its own. Across the lower Mekong's tributaries, more than one hundred dams are already up and running in Vietnam, Cambodia, Thailand, and Laos, and hundreds more have been proposed.[7]

Coupled with the changing climate, these dams are causing water levels in the Mekong to plummet. As the Mekong dips, so do its tributaries. In July 2020 the level of the Tonle Sap River was thirteen feet below average.[8] Lately, at its worst, so little water flows out of the Mekong into the Tonle Sap and up to the lake that the river may as well have stopped reversing course.

In some ways, it is a wonder the Mekong basin survived this long. In 1957—with the sponsorship of the United Nations—Cambodia, Vietnam, Laos, and Thailand created the Mekong Committee.[9] The body sought to survey the river and build the region's first hydroelectric dams in an effort to kickstart economic development. As the foreign aid race between the U.S., China, and the Soviet Union approached its apogee, America entered as a major backer—providing technical support along with nearly a fifth of the budget.[10] The Army Corps of Engineers drafted a plan of action and hydrologists began charting appropriate points for dams. Three locations on or near the Mekong were given top priority: Pa Mong, north of Vientiane; Sambor, near to Cambodia's border with Laos; and just past Phnom Penh's *chaktomuk* confluence, the Tonle Sap River. A fourth, at Stung Treng, near the Sambor, was later added to the list. By the late 1980s, models projected, these four megaprojects along with hundreds of smaller dams would be generating enough electricity to power the rapidly growing Mekong nations.

The river's brief reprieve came at the cost of the region. Even as the American war raged in Vietnam, American bombs fell on Laos and Cambodia, and American troops and money poured into Thailand, the Mekong Committee valiantly pushed forward, drafting new plans and surveying what they could. But after the Khmer Rouge takeover in 1975, when Cambodia went dark, the large projects couldn't legally proceed. In a joint declaration signed just months before Phnom Penh fell, the committee had flagged the Mekong mainstream as a "resource of common interest." No dams could be built without unanimous consent.[11]

Two decades later, the Mekong River Commission (MRC) was signed into being in 1995. By then the geopolitical and economic landscape of the region had shifted tremendously and it took years of intense negotiations to create the committee's modern iteration. Unlike its predecessor, the MRC is focused far more on management and conservation of the Mekong basin. And ultimately it is toothless. There is a consultation process in which impacted nations are encouraged to raise concerns over planned projects, but there are no repercussions for ignoring them. Laos has already built two dams on the mainstem, with plans for seven more, despite vociferous opposition from its downstream neighbors. In 2020 Cambodia did announce a decade-long postponement on building any mainstem dams, but only at the urging of a Japanese consultant[12]—not in response to the reams of MRC research showing the havoc the dams would wreak on Vietnam and Cambodia. Tributary dams, meanwhile, are still moving forward.

Activism comes naturally to An Socheat, who has been watching these waters for decades. Her father was a commune councillor in Prek Toal and she grew up helping him work in the community. Today she is a community leader employed by an environmental protection group.

"I was born here and lived here for more than thirty years." She gestures toward the houses along the banks: a row of long wooden rectangles, the roofs silver and brick-red. Some have been expanded out and out again, appendages of new rooms perched on yet more docking. Clothes dry on bamboo railings, potted plants sit beneath the windows; at one house, a length of tarp is rolled tight beneath the eaves—to be pulled down and lashed along the width of the entryway when the rains come.

"You can see that we have big houses here because in the past there was good fishing."

Those days are over. There's less fish, smaller fish, and everyone has to travel farther for their meager catch. What Socheat watches, these days, is how life is being siphoned from the Tonle Sap.

When I speak to her in March 2017 she has recently returned from Thailand, where she met with fishers from across the Mekong. There, she learned every community that relies on this river is facing similar problems. The droughts and the shallow water, the unceasing illegal fishing, and the dams: all of the Mekong's fisheries are being unmade in precisely the same manner.

Socheat came home and tried to impart this lesson: "Even though we are far from the Mekong, we are affected by its dams."

She has been teaching her neighbors how to fight against hydropower, how to join their voices with those across the Mekong basin. But she is also trying to get them funding to diversify their income: raising chickens, planting vegetables. She pushes for girls to go to school, tries to lessen the burdens that are contributing to a rise in domestic violence and alcoholism. She wants to offer training in vocational skills—tailoring, for instance.

Simply put, she wants to guide them to opportunities off the Tonle Sap. "I think in the future, some of them won't be fishers."

The situation on the lake seems entirely unsustainable. The life that once supported these large houses is fast failing.

"The poor families don't have enough food and they face malnutrition. Even when they can catch big fish, they sell that fish to the middleman and keep only the small fish to eat."

Socheat begins describing what life was like as a child. So much has been lost, it's hard to know where to start.

"Back then, when the water level rose in rainy season, the water was fresh. There was the river, the flooded forests, the birds, the streams. We used to have more than one hundred types of fish here."

Now, there's just the looming prospect of the Mekong being sealed off by dams, draining water from the Tonle Sap never to return it, leaving the lake without its pulse.

"My main concern is the dams. In the future, I'm not sure there will even be water here."

In July 2017 the village of Kbal Romeas is covered in graffiti—"NOLS2DAM" in English and Khmer—blue and white paint slashed menacingly across broad wood walls. In Stung Treng province, almost two hundred miles east from Prek Toal, a different riverside community has made this its protest anthem, painted on walls and trees, on houses and sheds.

At the height of rainy season, when the broad dirt road running through here becomes shoe-stealing thick, Kbal Romeas is striking. The houses are large, made of fine forest hardwood set on stilts one gentle flight above ground. Palms, frangipani, and fruit trees press against the village, dusky green and lush, perfuming the humid air. Twenty steps from the road, a verdant bank spills into a river swollen with the rains. Cross it with a slim, wooden boat and there are the farmlands, lousy with corn.

The river is the Srepok, and barely twenty miles away looms the source of the village protest: the Lower Sesan 2 dam, or LS2. The behemoth hydropower plant is set to go online in the coming months, submerging Kbal Romeas and neighboring villages that lie within the reservoir boundaries. Those living here are indigenous minorities: Bunong, Kuy, Lao. Their villages are set inside sacred forests and burial grounds. This land is their spirit, and they won't have it drowned without a fight.

Construction on the dam is long finished by now and its gates were recently closed for a test run. So Kbal Romeas has been pressing forward with a half-mad effort to save itself from the rising tides. In recent days, indigenous people from across Cambodia have been trickling into this remote village, offering their moral and physical support to fight the type of "development" project that has been displacing ethnic minorities from their ancestral lands nationwide. There have been meetings filled with stirring speeches by the visitors, some of whom have traveled more than a day by bus and motorcycle.

"People should be like the ant. When an ant sees food, he calls the others to help. We have to love each other and work together," one man offers, during a public talk. "Once the government can get this land, they'll move to another and another, until no one can live. So I want to urge people to work together. When I talk to people here, they say they're not moving out—if they die, they prefer to die here. Even if police shoot them, they're not moving out." The group roars with applause.

There have been discussions and planning and hard labor. Tall piles of freshly cut bamboo—rafts in the making—are stacked beneath many of the houses. If they can't beat the government and the company, residents have decided they will try the impossible and float their homes.

Police and soldiers are posted at the entrance to the small soggy road leading through the forest into Kbal Romeas, located about an hour away by motorbike during this season. They are polite but uneasy—this type of activism is dangerous. People coming together, it's like they're building a fire. My group gets past, only just, after villagers arrive to confront the police and insist we be let in. By the next day, tensions have risen further, and the village is effectively sealed off: other journalists and rights monitors are turned back. Sorry, but we do not want you to be burned, is what the presence of such authorities says.

Once the gates are fully closed in the coming months, hundreds of millions of gallons will pour into a twenty-nine-square-mile reservoir, wiping out the villages within. Already most residents have left. By the time the meetings are convened, some four thousand families in Kbal Romeas and neighboring Srekor village have agreed to be resettled on a spare, sandy plot near the national road—where the farmland is poor and security is heavy. Only a few hundred refuse to budge.

"I don't want to throw everything away," Srang Lang says. I meet her on the banks of the Srepok, where she is setting off for the farmlands. A handwoven basket is strapped to her back, a periwinkle hoodie staves off the drizzle. Lang has two gold teeth that glint in the light. When she speaks it is brusque and clear: "I don't need anything in exchange."

As recently as a few generations ago, elephants roamed here. Though they are long gone, this land is rich; it has managed to avoid the worst of the deforestation, soil degradation, and land grabs that have doomed so much of Cambodia's rural population in recent decades.

"My grandfather took one pair of tusks to give to King Sihanouk to get this land. The authorities made a commitment to him," Lang says.

Construction on the LS2 began in 2014. In the years since, fish catch has dropped by half, residents estimate. Lang turns to leave; she's in a rush—there are guests to be fed and the corn won't collect itself. "What happened to the fish?" I ask as she picks her way toward the river.

"When the dam gate is closed, the water goes up higher and stronger, that's why the fish can't come."

On maps, the LS2 dam is a ragged black line slicing across the Sesan River, right before it splits into the Srepok. A third river, the Sekong, carves off just downstream from the dam. These three "S" rivers make up a critical river basin extending to Vietnam and Laos and are considered key tributaries of the Mekong.

In aerial photos, the reservoir behind the LS2 looks like twin dragons spreading out from the Sesan and Srepok. The dam itself is more than four miles across, making it one of the longest in the world. It has been almost a decade since scientists calculated exactly how catastrophic it will be to switch off this particular ecosystem. All dams block fish migration pathways and cause siltation upstream and nutrient loss downstream. Located barely twenty miles west of the Mekong, the LS2 is a master offender. Modeling suggests that within a few years this dam will lead to a 9.3 percent drop in fish across the lower Mekong basin—four times the loss caused by the second-most impactful tributary dam.[13]

There have been protests against the LS2 ever since it was first proposed in 2009: marches and petitions, impassioned letters to leaders. Residents have tried black magic, holding ceremonies to curse the developers.[14] Punish them with bankruptcy, they begged of the spirits, force them to stop. Like the scientists, fishers have been keenly aware of how this dam will destroy their ability to survive.

Still, the government has forged ahead.

The LS2 has been held up by Cambodian officials as an essential project for development. More than a third of the nation's electricity is imported, and a significant portion of its population is not yet connected to the grid or suffers frequent power outages. In its strategic plans, the Cambodian government vowed nationwide electrification by 2020 (and came close) with 70 percent of rural homes directly hooked up by 2030. Between the growth in factories, construction, and mass electrification, the demand for power has been increasing at almost 20 percent a year for the past decade and is expected to grow more than sevenfold between 2015 and 2040.[15] Accordingly, Cambodia has undertaken a major push to increase native electricity generation—primarily through coal-fired plants and hydropower.

The $816 million LS2 dam is a pillar of that program and a symbol of Cambodia's development strategy. A joint venture between a Chinese state-held company and Cambodia's Royal Group, which is owned by one of the country's most powerful tycoons, the LS2 represents the biggest hydropower project to date. For the next four decades, Électricité du Cambodge, Cambodia's state-run electricity company, will purchase electricity from the owners. If the company cannot pay, the Cambodian government will.[16]

The government took on this financial gamble in the hopes of meeting the needs of a rapidly industrializing country. Growing sporelike on the outskirts of every Cambodian city, garment factories have become a linchpin of the economy. But who wants to sink money into a factory that must pause for hours when electricity is scarce?

"The dam will help the government to distribute electricity to develop the country. The electricity will attract investors to invest in factories,"

Suy Sem, minister of industry, mines, and energy, said in 2013 after the ruling party voted to approve the risky financial guarantees.[17] "I am confident that electricity in Cambodia will be improved."

In this way, the LS2 is very much like the rest of the dams mushrooming across the lower Mekong and its tributaries—defended as necessary to grow economies and increase development. Energy demand for the lower Mekong basin is projected to rise by 6 to 7 percent annually, and hydropower has long been a cornerstone of regional development plans. The planned mainstem hydropower projects total almost 13,000 MW and cost nearly $30 billion. Another thirty dams planned on major Mekong tributaries have a capacity of more than 10,000 MW at a cost of $20.6 billion. If all the mainstem dams are built, they may meet an estimated 6 to 8 percent of the lower Mekong basin's energy needs. By 2040, officials are fond of touting, the lower Mekong basin could see economic gains of more than $160 billion.[18]

While the Cambodian government crows about the benefits of the dams, the trade-off is steep and, by now, remarkably well documented. Recent modeling by the MRC has shown precisely the ways in which food insecurity will rise, flood damage will worsen, and the "effects of poverty will remain."[19]

The decline of fisheries could cost the region nearly $23 billion by 2040. The loss of forests, wetlands, and mangroves may cost up to $145 billion. With more than 90 percent of sedimentation blocked, rice growth along the Mekong will be severely affected. Fish farms, irrigation schemes, and agricultural projects could help offset these losses—but with uneven results between classes and countries. Because it is so far downstream and lacks the economic cushion and strong governance of neighboring Vietnam, Cambodia will suffer these impacts more than any other Mekong nation. "Cambodia is likely to experience from a national perspective the highest trade-off: for every dollar gained from hydropower about 62 cents would be lost in fisheries," noted an MRC report.[20]

Hunger will rise, instability will grow. Poverty is set to increase, not shrink.

The LS2 went fully online in December 2018. Within two months, a prolonged drought had rendered the dam useless and power cuts roiled much of Cambodia for months. Tens, if not hundreds, of millions of dollars were lost. Perhaps it was the curse.

The dam has split Sah Voeurn's family. Two of his children and two of his siblings remain in Srekor village. Three kids and four siblings have moved to the relocation site along the national road. He shuttles back and forth—two hours at the height of the rainy season, when the roads have grown so muddy a tractor is the best way to travel. When I meet him outside the Kbal Romeas meeting house, Voeurn is dressed in a pink button-down shirt and charcoal trousers, his hems lightly spattered with mud. He's come to this neighboring village for the talks and ceremony, eager to learn how best to fight the looming tide.

The government says dams are needed for development. Voeurn's smile is wide, he laughs that off.

"The government is building the dam to get more income for the government, not for the villagers. The villagers get poorer and poorer and the money that comes in just goes to the government," he says. "It's development according to one person. The people in urban areas can't live without electricity. The people here can live without electricity, but we can't live without fishing, land, and animals."

Around us, rain is weeping into the soil and overflowing broad ceramic water jugs. A piglet wobbles by.

"For them, it's useful, but for us—we just want our land."

Downriver from Kbal Romeas is Koh Preah, a bucolic island village about one hundred miles due east of the lake. Kbal Romeas lies on the shores of the Srepok, but Koh Preah is nestled in the Mekong itself, one of dozens of sandy stretches that sit just below the confluence of the three S rivers. When the waters rush in and out of the Tonle Sap Lake, this is the route migrating fish are following. They come down the Tonle Sap River and up the Mekong, swimming past this pretty village, with its packed red roads and palm trees, wooden bridges, and thatched homes. It is here where the nooses are tightening.

"People in rural areas like this, our main food is fish. When they build the hydropower dam, it means that they kill us," says Thit Poeung, a forty-year-old father of five who has spent his whole life on this island.

People in this part of Cambodia tend to know about hydropower because they are surrounded by it. Thirty miles in any direction sits a proposed dam, a dam under construction, or a completed hydropower project. The LS2, northeast of here, is only the start. Due north on the Mekong, just over the Lao border, lies the Don Sahong dam. The 260-megawatt project broke ground in January 2016 and went online almost four years later—despite significant outcry from neighboring governments. Halfway between the Lao border and this island stands the site of the proposed Stung Treng dam. Farther downriver is where the planned Sambor dam might be placed. Though both projects have been paused for a decade, combined they could total nearly three thousand megawatts—dwarfing other lower Mekong dams.[21]

Like their counterparts on the Tonle Sap Lake and near the three "S" rivers, Mekong fishers hardly need economic impact research to confirm what they see with their own eyes.

Cheam So Phat, a studious thirty-seven-year-old, is one among hundreds in Koh Preah who have begun migrating to survive. Both Phat and his younger brother worked for years as factory and plantation laborers in Thailand before returning home, hoping to figure out a way to stay put. The undocumented work paid enough to live, not save, but that's more than he has been able to find in his village.

"We've lost the forest and we've lost river resources. They were the main source for us to earn a living and to eat. Now you have lost this stuff—how could you survive in the future?"

While Phat speaks, he mends a fishing net. The Mekong—just yards from his house—used to teem with fish. In recent years, the catch has dropped precipitously. If there is a development angle to hydropower, says Phat, it is not one that touches his life.

"I've heard about the project to build the hydropower dam, but I don't know how the word *development* is connected," he says. Day by day, he observes the precise opposite: destruction.

"I know when there is meant to be more fish and when there is meant to be less fish. If it's past the high season and there's still less fish, that means they closed the dam, they turned the water system off—the water level isn't changing, and the fish aren't coming. Before, in the dry season you get less fish because there is low water, and in the rainy season you get more fish. But now, in every season you get less fish."

The big fish are gone, but at least the little fish are doing just fine: this, for the longest time, seemed to be the received wisdom on the Tonle Sap. But lately, ever so anecdotally, some are seeing even the trey riel catch dropping. The dams, the droughts—the dangerous combination of the two are beginning to affect Cambodia's most important fish.

It's March 2017 and Him Tash is standing on her boat, a few miles from Kampong Prek, pulling at a sopping net twisted with trey riel. Behind her, the Tonle Sap is a flat unfurling of brown, its surface pocked with tiny waves. Three other fishers, hats pulled low against the glare, stand in the water. The lake laps at their chests while they work.

"In previous years, there were many more fish than this," Tash says, untangling the net and pulling out the tiny silver bodies with a practiced hand.

The fishers take turns standing in the water. One slowly walks an end of the netting out and out until it forms a giant circle; the others slap sticks against the lake's surface, sending frenzied cyprinids into the net. They do this over and over, for the whole of the morning and early afternoon. The group, neighbors from the same village, are rice farmers who grow enough only to feed themselves. During the dry season, fishing for trey riel is how these farmers get by. They bring it home, make prahok, and sell some for extra income. "I don't think we could support ourselves only from the farm," Tash says.

She pulls, and pulls, long fingers gathering the net in folds, water dripping down her flowered pants. The trey riel seem impossibly few—lengths of netting between each silver flash.

"I'm concerned," she says, frowning at the pitiful haul. "If we can't catch fish, we can't make money."

FIG. I. Workers load a family's fishing boat onto a truck bound for Vietnam in 2016. Courtesy of Nicolas Axelrod/Ruom.

FIG. 2. Mending fishing nets in Prek Toal. Courtesy of Nicolas Axelrod/Ruom.

FIG. 3. An aerial shot of Kampong Luong floating village. Courtesy of Nicolas Axelrod/Ruom.

FIG. 4. Workers pull in trey riel at a dai fishery. Courtesy of Nicolas Axelrod/Ruom.

FIG. 5. Laborers unload baskets of fish at a market at Kampong Khleang village. Courtesy of Nicolas Axelrod/Ruom.

FIG. 6. A fishing family on the Tonle Sap. Courtesy of Nicolas Axelrod/Ruom.

FIG. 7. Waiting to fish in the rainy season. Courtesy of Nicolas Axelrod/Ruom.

FIG. 8. Prahok makers shovel partially fermented trey riel into buckets as part of a wholesale operation. Courtesy of Nicolas Axelrod/Ruom.

FIG. 9. Vendors travel by boat through Kampong Luong floating village. Courtesy of Nicolas Axelrod/Ruom.

FIG. 10. Lunchtime in Kampong Prek floating village. Courtesy of Nicolas Axelrod/ Ruom.

FIG. 11. A family pulls their house farther out toward the Tonle Sap Lake as water levels remain abnormally low during rainy season 2019. Courtesy of Nicolas Axelrod/ Ruom.

5 When the Water Recedes, the Ant Eats the Fish

The bottom of the lake is a swirl of tributaries and inlets, spilling across paddy fields and twisting back into the Tonle Sap River like so much merging traffic. Along a sandy shore here in Kampong Chhnang province is a small wholesale fish market set on a raised slab of concrete overlooking a ferry port and a clutch of tumbling bankside homes.

It's a pleasant morning at the start of rainy season, cloudy and cool, a slight breeze ruffling the murky water. Storm clouds are gathering in the distance—low steel streaks against the rolling green of the marshland opposite—and the shoppers are moving briskly. A group of middlemen in camo pants and khaki shorts makes their way past a line of colorful plastic baskets heaped to the tops: black gills slick with water and blood. A woman in a faded orange blouse, a thin gold chain draped around her neck, studies her ledger.

Here, an inversion: fish comes from the land and goes out to the water. A vendor pulls up in her boat and buys a few pounds of snakehead fish to sell in the floating villages. "There's not many fish on the river, I just get it from the farm," she explains.

The market opens early and by midday, the sellers have packed up and gone home. As they leave, Eam Darai hoses down the platform. He is tall, with perfect posture and wears a faded red krama draped neatly around his neck. At sixty-two, Darai has worked at this port for a third of his life.

"When I first came here, it was all fresh fish," he says. "All the snake-heads you see here now are farmed. There's a lot of fishing now, that's why the number has declined." Are there other causes? "You better ask the fishermen. We live along the mainland and don't know much about that."

More than electricity, factories, development, or growth, what the seventy million people living in the lower Mekong basin need is food. In a decade, that population may reach as high as one hundred million, and their survival is tightly wound up with the river system in which they live.[1] Rice is what is grown on the floodplain; fish is what is cultivated in the waterways. These two foods are the most fundamental staples here, and the troubles facing the Mekong badly threaten both. If, after time immemorial, food will not come from its natural source—where can it be had?

Pursat province's Road 54 spools out from the lake's southern third like a plumb bob, widening from a muddy red strip into concrete, skirting farmland and villages. Lining the road, jostling up against one another in squares of emerald, cobalt, and jade, sit the fish farms of Krakor.

If the fish are vanishing from the lake, they're multiplying in pools like these across the country. The farms represent the most modern iteration of a millennia-old practice of storing, breeding, and growing freshwater fish. On the lake, fish is farmed under or alongside homes in hatcheries made of wood and wire. On land, fish is grown in ponds that can take the form of anything from small backyard endeavors to mechanized lots many acres in size.

There are few industries here that have grown at the rate of aquaculture. In 1984 Cambodia produced about sixteen hundred tons of farmed fish.[2] In 2019 that figure surpassed three hundred thousand tons.[3] When the vendors row their skiffs through the floating villages, bearing incongruous bags of fish for sale—this is what they're selling.

But while these fish farms help solve one problem, they are also hastening the disappearance of the Tonle Sap's fish.

There are many families of fish that farmers can grow, but there is only one most anybody wishes to: trey ros, or snakehead fish. The common snakehead in particular is one of the most reliably popular species, a mainstay of soups and steamers. Snakeheads are, by some counts, ten times more profitable than other farmed fish.[4] Rapacious carnivores, snakeheads eat everything. And the easiest thing to feed them has always been smaller fish.

As fish farms proliferated during the 1990s and 2000s, fishers ravaged the lake seeking wild fingerlings to keep up with the demand. A single farm pond requires several tons of small feed fish over the eight months in which the snakeheads grow to full size.[5] Fearing the lake would soon be depleted of juvenile fish—both for food and for stocking the ponds—the government banned snakehead farming in 2004. Though the ban was born of genuine ecological concern, there is little indication it had the intended effect. Neighboring Vietnam still allowed the farming of snakeheads, so there remained a sizable market for small fish. And while the restrictions lasted more than a decade, enforcement was scarce. When the government legalized snakehead farming again in 2016, officials cited the wide availability of commercial feed.[6] Still, any number of farmers find it easier to rely on the lake's natural supply.

A propaganda poet wrote in 1982, three years after the fall of the brutal Khmer Rouge regime:

Fish, fish, fish
all over the water, mud, and land.
Too many fish to eat
too many different kinds.
There's no lack.

Years of starvation, forced labor, and endless death came to an end, replaced, wrote civil servant Sar Kapun, by a government as giving as the Great Lake. His poem "Our Boeung Tonle Sap" detailed the double movement of the river, the never-ending pulse that fed a nation.

Tonle Sap Lake.
In dry season, there is the strong smell of

delicious and plentiful fish
for feeding our children
and increasing our people.
Cambodia develops without
worrying about food to eat.
In rainy season
crystal clear waters flow in
to fill up the lake.
The water looks massively full.
Oh, lake, please
take good care.[7]

There are a pair of turquoise rectangles behind Hieng Ty Hung's house, their corners neatly squared off, the water glassy with little hint of the thousands of snakeheads living below the surface. Ty Hung and her husband, Sok Py, moved here a decade earlier from the nearby floating village of Kampong Luong, watching as their neighbors followed suit, one by one.

"The number of people who rent fish farms has really gone up. In the past, there were just a few here, now there are more than twenty," Ty Hung tells me in 2017.

The economics of fish farming are tricky, a constant gamble, the couple explains. Lower prices from Vietnam, where rumor has it they use hormones to make their fish grow faster, cut into a farmer's profit. A bad flood, like in 2012, can sweep away a whole season's worth of fish. If the middleman shows up too late, there goes yet more profit. Then, too, the price of tiny feed fish always seems to be rising.

"In the past, small fish cost one thousand riel for a kilo, now it's fifteen hundred," says Py. "The fisheries officials are strict about catching the small fish, so the price goes up," his wife adds.

The economics of the floating village worked no better—even a decade earlier, fishing was a beggar's game.

"We moved here because we were banned from fishing with our equipment," Py explains. He pauses to clarify. The bans make sense, he understands the impetus, but they simply do not work. The water keeps dropping and there seems to be no more fish.

"I still fish sometimes. I use different types of nets to catch the small fish to feed the fish in our farm. But now, they restrict us from fishing. And they only allow us to use equipment that can't catch fish," he says. "I think the fish must have gone to other countries. If there's no water, how can the fish live here?"

Fish farms are the solution to the dying lake. Or at least, this is what everyone seems to think. In June 2020 Prime Minister Hun Sen delivered a speech at the country's Freshwater Aquaculture Research and Development Center.[8] "We cannot rely on fishery products from a lack of river anymore. We need to promote the aquatic sector, grow more, raise more animals and process food to export," he told a crowd of fish farmers.

While freshwater fish catch dropped 14 percent from 2019 to 2020, the amount collected from aquaculture grew by nearly a third.[9] The fish farms produced four hundred forty thousand tons, nearly equivalent to what was pulled from the rivers and the Tonle Sap that year.

Thinny Sothy, a fisheries official in Siem Reap, insists that the government intends to move lake dwellers en masse and teach them how to grow fish from the land. The U.S. government has launched a $17 million fish farming project.[10] The UN calls aquaculture the answer to food insecurity. A few years back, a Chinese firm and its Cambodian partner announced a $100 million fish farm.[11]

Let's face it, the Tonle Sap is finished, these projects seem to say. It's time to move on.

Van Voeun is dressed in an oversized army jacket, sleeves rolled past his wrists. Smile lines pull at his eyes and a flop of curly hair, cut close at the sides, tumbles across his forehead. At forty-three, Voeun has lived on the lake his whole life and watched it shrink before his eyes. Can his five children continue in this profession? Each year that seems less likely. The steps leading up to his home in Kampong Khleang are like a ladder, and he tucks himself into a lower rung before lighting a cigarette and continuing his train of thought.

"There's been a big change. This time of year, in the dry season, there isn't usually strong wind, but it's become very common now. In the past, it was easy to fish during the dry season, but now it's difficult because the wind is so strong."

In 2017, though, there are bigger problems. "I think if the government doesn't crack down on illegal fishing, the fish will keep declining." Corruption seems rampant. Villagers complain that some fisheries officials sell their old uniforms to civilians who extort money from fishers. When the genuine officers are out, they seem to focus on tiny cases: someone who cut a small branch for her traps, someone who fished with the wrong type of net. They're rarely going after the prime offenders, as evinced, says Voeun, by the fact that "now there are many fisheries officials on the lake, but the fish keep declining."

So Voeun's business these days is selling feed fish. "I catch small fish to sell to the middleman to raise big fish," he explains. "It's used as food for snakeheads." On a good day, Voeun can catch about $10 worth of the finger-length trey changvar. On a bad day, it's more like $5.

Like other snakehead feed fishers here, Voeun sells his catch to buyers from nearby Siem Reap city, who gather the little fish pound by pound and sell it on to the fish farms across the province. He thinks it can't be illegal, since what he does is on such a small scale. Plus, what other fish could he be netting nowadays?

"I only catch small fish because I don't have the equipment for big fish," he says. "I don't want to use illegal methods because I'm concerned that in the future the number of fish will drop."

Two boats pull into the inlet in Kampong Khleang. The fish filling their hulls are smaller than a thumb, soft and silvery, white bellies pinkening in the air. A teenager in an Adidas T-shirt and white jeans scoops out the catch with his long-necked pole, tipping each bulging netful into a hamper. A pair of workers drag the baskets up the bank, pausing to heave them on a scale before setting them in neat rows in front of Chhlounh Samlang.

She's the impresario here, presiding over an empire of tiny fish. When each briny basket arrives, Samlang scrawls the weight in her ledger. She and the rest of the buyers are dressed for business in turtlenecks or scarves, sleeves that shade their wrists from the sun, fingerless gloves and sandal-socks cleaved neatly at the big toe. A purse—fat with money—hangs at each waist. As they glide among the men and the fish, the boats and the baskets and the scales, the women scratch at their notebooks, setting neat lines of figures marching down the pages.

The fish coming in today are mostly trey riel. But while the other women are selling their hauls to prahok makers, this dealer runs a different sort of enterprise.

"I buy small fish and sell to a middleman who sells them to be fed to big fish," says Samlang.

In the little man-made ponds encircling the Tonle Sap, snakeheads are plumping up on Cambodia's nutrient-rich staple. Once the lumbering trey ros are nice and fat, they'll be sold at a price many times higher per pound than that of trey riel, to a different, wealthier customer.

Even as the lake is struggling, even as the catch is dropping and the fishermen are making less than they ever have, this type of business has stayed steady, Samlang tells me. She loans money to the fishers, who use it to pay for new equipment and repairs—then sell their fish to her at a lower price. Ten people work for her, day laborers who haul the heavy baskets of fish. Each day, Samlang buys and sells around eighteen hundred pounds. In the rainy season, that figure tops twenty-two hundred. In March 2017 tremors on the Tonle Sap have not yet touched this market; it's still booming. Small fish is where the money is now, Samlang says. As long as these can be had in abundance it's less hassle, less risk.

The whole time we talk, her men are pulling baskets up to the shore, calling out the weight, and loading one after another onto a trailer attached to a motorbike. Each basket weighs about one hundred pounds and in short order they've loaded eleven onto just one middleman's cart.

"I used to be a fisher," she tells me. The whole time she talks, she keeps one eye trained sharply on her workers. "Changing from fisher to buyer is a good move."

It's morning at Siem Reap's Psar Leur and the market is jumping. Stalls here have everything a shopper from the mainland or the lake could need: tamarinds fat in their pods, bottles of whitening moisturizer, cheery purple bags of detergent powder, and crusty baguettes. There is a section for meat and a section for vegetables, and then, under a universe of makeshift canopies draped across metal poles: the fish. Bags of fish heads and piles of freshly gutted carp, stacks of dried silver barb and listless live catfish packed into broad metal boxes. Shoppers stroll by, wallets at the ready, bending to inspect a shell, to prod at a gill.

The snakeheads at Eang Srey Neang's stand don't come from the Tonle Sap. "It comes from the ponds. In general, there's not much of this kind that is freshly caught." The vendor has little hope that will change in the coming years. Mat Ly, for his part, estimates perhaps 80 percent of his sales are farmed fish. "Fish farming is really increasing. I think the number of fish in the lake are declining," he says. Once, Ly worked as a fisherman. Selling—farmed or fresh from the lake—is so much easier it could barely be compared. "Working as a fisherman is very difficult," he says. Worse by the year.

A customer wanders down a market laneway. Draped off her wrist is a plastic bag holding a large, bloody fish. Neth Thida has no favorite fish, "as long as it's fresh."

She tells us how to spot the difference, swears that the farmed ones are redder beneath the gills. The fresh fish tastes so much more delicious and is less likely to be pumped full of chemicals that speed its growth. It's something worth paying more for, when she can afford to do so.

"I think fresh fish is much better, but farmed fish is so much cheaper."

Sok Keo, still in debt from his descent into the conservation zone, is adamant his children have a better life than his. If the family could just leave their floating home in Kampong Prek, everything would improve.

He seems almost buoyant as he outlines his hopes. His kids could get some opportunities, things would change. He knows, too, precisely what he would do if he got to move to land. He would dig a pond and build a fish farm. As the fisherman sees it, this type of business is precisely the key to survival.

"That's why we want to live on the mainland. I want to send them to school so they can find different jobs and don't have to be fishers."

6 *Do Not Rely on the God of Mercy*

One morning in 2019, I open a satellite map of the Tonle Sap on my computer and click my way around it. The water is a milky brown and at various points I can spot the floating villages if I squint and keep my eyes sharp. They look even more precarious in this digital soup than they do up close. A few dozen homes here and there, pinpricks against the lake's great expanse.

To live in a floating home is to live in a constant state of flux. The materials are all land-born: wood and corrugated aluminum, rubber tires and plastic barrels, rope used in limitless ingenious ways. But beneath one's feet is the constant feel of nothing. The steady roll of water reminds at once how much and how little there is. We have this whole lake, a floating house says with each gentle thrall to the tide. We have nothing.

In a country full of poor, very poor, and severely impoverished people, many of those on the lake feel they sit at the bottom. If a farmer has a plot of land that never quite yields enough, that is constantly in danger of being grabbed by someone richer and more powerful—well, she has earth beneath her feet. She has collateral to take out another usurious microfinance loan. She has a dirt path that leads to a small road that leads to a bigger one that leads to a school, a market, a health clinic.

"Being a farmer is much easier than being a fisher," an elderly man named Sen Mat tells me one cloudy March morning. Each year Mat and his wife and some of their neighbors set up a sort of temporary camp on a southern Tonle Sap bank that remains grassy even at the height of dry season. This marshland lies nestled between two floating villages, a mile from each set of bobbing homes, grass spreading lichenlike across its sandy surface. When the pastures in nearby Krakor turn brown and dry in the heat, the group leads their oxen here to feed. Their shelters are made of tarps and sticks punched into the soft earth, tiny waves lapping at the stilts. Behind them, the lake ranges endless as an ocean. Mat fishes near these banks and grows rice near his inland home. He holds no envy for those who have only the lake to rely on.

A floating village can take many forms. Some floating houses sit on large, square-hulled barges. The bottoms are broad, made of quality wood slung low in the water. When waves sweep the lake, these barges roll gracefully as a boxer. The roofs are solid, the living quarters large and well-apportioned. To be sure, this does not make for an easy life. Those living on big boats face many of the same privations as any of their floating neighbors; few farmers would trade their humble fields for these houseboats. But most who live on the lake fare far worse. The simplest homes in a floating village are something of a marvel: how do they survive the water and wind? These houses have thin wood floors lashed raftlike to tires and fifty-gallon plastic barrels. The walls are made of salvaged wood or corrugated tin. They're layered with green tarp or strips of palm leaf tied neatly down—the shaggy coat soon patchy.

Kampong Prek sits near the mouth of a nameless river on the lake's southern edge and is filled with these types of homes. Here, just sixty-three houses float within shouting distance of one another. When the lake swells with rain, residents row their homes inland, always hugging a shore. To call it a village seems an exaggeration. There is no shop or school or medical center, just a few dozen families trying very hard, and mostly failing, to get by. What ties people here together the most? A wild, all-consuming desire to move to land.

Mok Hien is seventy-one and has lived most of his life in houses like these: wood, tarp, barrels; roofs that send rain cascading across the floor; walls that let gales scream on through. He has been in Kampong

Prek since the fall of the Khmer Rouge in 1979 and has four children and sixteen grandchildren. Most live nearby, but some have begun to leave—to Battambang, to Phnom Penh, to the cities where a semblance of opportunity exists.

Hien's glasses are Coke-bottle thick; his hair is a shock of black, trimmed short in the back. He wears a krama wrapped tightly about his waist and pulls a T-shirt over his head while we wait to speak with him. His wife sits nearby, confusion sparking across her face. His daughter bounces a cheerful baby boy—half of a pair of yellow-shirted twins.

The family is tired because the night before a storm rolled into Krakor district, lashing the lake. My colleagues and I watched transfixed from the comfort of our rooms in a concrete guesthouse just a few miles inland. At roughly the same time, Hien and his children were standing in the knee-deep water, anchoring their home with their bodies so it wouldn't blow over.

"The wind is getting stronger and stronger, and I was afraid the house would collapse," Hien explains.

Hien begins telling us the type of story that's like a fairy tale for the poorest—it's the balm politicians promise for wounds, even when what is needed is medicine, stitches, surgery. There's land about a mile away, and it could be theirs. All five dozen families have made an official request for the available plot. If the ruling party wins the next local election, the land is theirs—so says the commune chief. Of course they will vote for their shot at moving off the lake.

"All of the people here have asked the authorities for land to build houses and to plant crops. But there's been no result yet. We requested it twice already, in 2016 and 2017. They told us to wait until after the commune council election. The commune chief said if the CPP wins, we'll get it. So, yes. I'll vote for the CPP."

Such deals are commonplace here, where Prime Minister Hun Sen's ruling Cambodian People's Party (CPP) has maintained an unbroken winning streak through brute force and shining promises. Come election time, local leaders make the rounds, handing out kramas and bags of rice, small amounts of cash and the odd meal. Ruling party hats, T-shirts, and stickers litter the countryside for years after—at times it seems every other old man is dressed in a CPP shirt or cap. Though it is less effective these days, the party has long campaigned on threats, warning of a return to civil war that resonates with the traumatized older population. "Who saved you from the Khmer Rouge?" the CPP still likes to remind voters. Who built hospitals and schools? Who brought the country back from Year Zero? The threats are packaged with promises grand and small: new health centers and roads, new irrigation systems, new crackdowns on corruption, on crime, on whatever may trouble a particular village.

Real land in exchange for ownerless water: A bold promise, to be sure, but who wouldn't take the chance and cast their ballot for the CPP?

Hien tells me more about Kampong Prek's dreamland. It is available because it is part forest and part Vietnamese graveyard.

"The Vietnamese forced the Khmer to move away. Now the Khmer forces the Vietnamese ghosts to move away." Hien's face cracks apart in delight at his dark joke.

After last night's storm, a rare cool breeze cuts through the March heat. Outside Hien's house, the lake is becalmed now. Beneath the hazy sky, the water in these churned shallows is nearly opaque: a crumpled reflection below each home.

From Hien's deck, I can see his neighbors sculling their boats through the village. Some are returning with the day's scant catch; others are heading out. Parents are rinsing out pans, children cleaning rice for dinner. How many of them stood in the lake a night earlier, holding up their failing homes, I wonder. How many saw the wind damage a wall there is no money to repair? How many coughs for which there is no medicine?

"Things are different from last year. The lake has never been like this before," Hien tells me. The forest fires and the heat of 2016 had driven people near the edge. The powerful gusts from the newly exposed lake are pushing them still closer. Hien is certain it's only a matter of time—years? months? weeks?—before the gales grow so strong they collapse his home. The houses here seem terribly exposed to the larger forces. In a corner of Hien's house that doubles as a kitchen, pot lids are tucked neatly inside the wall frames and a pan hangs from a hook; a rooster moves lustily across the worn floor. If the storms become more powerful, could any of this be saved?

Hien points out that moving to the land won't just save the hungry fishing families—it could well save the fish.

"If the government moves people who live here, in two or three years, you'll see a lot of fish," he predicts. "When we came back after three years of the Khmer Rouge, there were lots of fish here. Now, we can't even find one."

Hien rhapsodizes about learning to farm. He is old, but not too old to pick up a new skill. And then there are the children, and those who come after them.

"I want to live on the mainland. I think the next generation will too."

In 1929 a French civil servant and polymath named George Groslier began venturing out from Phnom Penh along the Mekong and its tributaries on a multiyear project to document Cambodia's Buddhist pagodas. An artist and a writer, Groslier possessed a sharp eye for detail and an open-minded exuberance deeply wanting among the colonial class.

En route up the Tonle Sap River from Phnom Penh, Groslier paused about halfway to the lake, not far from Cambodia's former capital Oudong. There, at the river's bank, he contemplated the fisheries that had been laid out along the upper Tonle Sap.[1]

"They have just been set up and will multiply up to the Great Lake. I stopped counting them yesterday. What is a fishery in Cambodia, at this season, on the Tonlé Sap?" Groslier is awed by the scene. "I have been dazzled by strange visions, by I know not what chaos of mercury, mother-of-pearl, and steel, and human bodies dipping into it with muddled gestures."

Similar to today's dai fisheries, the ones Groslier documented had emerged during dry season at strategic points along the Tonle Sap. Rattan screens were suspended in the river and slowly dragged ever closer to push the migrating fish inside. The water within "boils, flashes, and bursts" with fish, their mass of writhing bodies drawn tighter. Men, women, children, "this entire Annamite world" drew up to empty the catch. "They toss a sturdy cylindrical basket to the men still in the fishery," writes Groslier. "These take it by the handles, plunge it in, and with monstrous effort pull it back out. It vibrates and blazes while other men take hold, and in one swoop thirty kilos of fish roll into the skiff. In half an hour the skiff is full, sunk to the gunwales under an agonizing, animate mass. Another skiff pulls up. And while this impoverishment of the river proceeds, I think of the hundred other fisheries just like this one operating at this very hour, stretching all the way to the lake a hundred kilometers away."

If this was the state of the fisheries shortly before Hien was born, it is almost unfathomable how far it could fall in the course of one man's life. Less, still, that it could unspool in such a way over just a handful of decades.

"It's impossible it will improve. It's just going to be less and less and worse and worse," Hien told me in 2016. "Honestly, if some NGO or the government provided us with one or two hectares, everyone here would go and live on land."

When we leave Hien, we drive north for another couple of miles, cutting near the shore—a thin tract of pale grass set against the fatter, darker tree line. The sky is crystalline by now, cloud streaks shredding across its crown. After twenty minutes we reach Akol, an even smaller version of its neighbor. A few dozen homes float here: green and silver corrugate walls set in wood frames, small boats tied to their supports. At the village edge, a slip of land emerges from the water, covered in shrubs and grass, a pair of buffalo grazing near the sandy shore. A man walks toward the bank, feet slapping at the muck.

Keng Sreymom comes from a fishing family. From the front of her floating home, she runs a small shop. Plastic bags, each filled with a few ounces of oil or sugar or roasted peanuts or salt, tied with long white threads, hang in clusters from neat lines of nails. Single-use sachets of shampoo and conditioner are strung from another wall above an assortment of soda cans and jugs of coffee. A neighbor rests against the wall, legs stretched against the smooth floorboards, sipping a lime-green drink.

"It's difficult to earn a living now," Sreymom says. "Sometimes we can't even make ten thousand riel a day. My husband is a fisherman, and he's out fishing. But this is just a small shop. Some customers pay, but some owe me money."

Sreymom's hair is pulled back in a tight ponytail and her eyes narrow as she speaks, pointedly, about the shortfalls of the government. She herself is a village chief, an elected local leader, but three years in office have done little to bolster her faith. The catch has grown abysmal, plundered by the large trawlers and rampant illegal fishing. Still, year after year, nothing is implemented that might better their lot.

"Honestly, the officials are just cracking down to save face, to not lose their jobs. It seems like they have no real willingness to do it well."

While Sreymom talks, she works a hand-cranked sugar cane juicer, spilling the honey-colored liquid into a baggie fat with ice, yanking a rubber band taut against the straw with a swift finger. She hands the makeshift cup to a customer, takes his tattered riels.

Born and raised in this village, Sreymom has seen its population balloon. "I think only about five families lived here then," she says. The neighbor pipes in: "Because everyone here has eight kids."

"There's a big problem with the fishing now," Sreymom continues. "We can't catch fish well. There's a few reasons. First, natural disasters. Second, there's a big increase in the number of families. There were only a few families here in the 1980s. Now, there's more than thirty. Third, now there's a lot of modern equipment used for fishing. There's electricity, trawlers, long nets—more than a kilometer long."

Since her election three years earlier, Sreymom has been pressing the government to award her community a social land concession—a rare type of public land scheme for the poor. As in Kampong Prek, people here just want to leave.

"We don't care where we go. Anywhere they give us, we will accept," Sreymom says.

Instead, the officials stall and stall. People like her, it seems, will never be a priority—not as long as land is valuable and buyers are eager.

"They just say they are considering giving it to us. But I think most of the land they'll turn into economic land concessions because these companies will pay the state for it. A few years ago, I requested to get land, but they said they couldn't. And then, they gave it to an investor."

Almost due north from these watery homes, forty-five miles across the Tonle Sap, lie Kampong Khleang and the rest of Siem Reap's bloated stilt communities. In the rainy season, the lake engulfs this area, spawning floating villages of another ilk. Houses here crowd against one another, long-legged spiders jostling for air. Lining the northern cusp of the lake as it edges toward Siem Reap city, these villages have spread like moss in recent years—new houses cropping up in seemingly every spare space.

The expansion hints at the rapid growth of lake communities. Between 2008 and 2019, the population density of the Tonle Sap region grew by a quarter, nearly twice the overall national rate.[2] Some 4.8 million people, almost one-third of Cambodia's total population, live in the "Tonle Sap region," which is made up of six provinces surrounding the lake. And while there are no precise figures on lake dwelling populations, researchers estimate two million Cambodians today depend on the lake directly for their work.[3]

The attraction is clear. Here are communities close to both the lake and a city; here lies a sense of possibility and expanded opportunity. But those living here rely no less heavily on fishing than their floating neighbors. Here too, all are failing to get by and aching to push farther inland.

A group of fishers sits beneath a stilt house in Kampong Khleang, repairing and trading stories of how bad the catch has been. When the lake floods, Kampong Khleang transforms into a floating village—water seeps higher and higher until it laps at the upper steps of the houses and boats are needed to move through the streets. Now, in dry season, life takes place between the stilts, under the shade of the looming homes. Though the village is less than an hour's drive from Siem Reap city, it's a world apart.

Most anyone here would leave if they could—but without fish there's no money, and without money, how could anyone ever obtain farmland?

"I wish I could quit fishing, but I have no money and nowhere to go," says Roan Sy, a thirty-six-year-old who has spent his life on these waters. "Some kinds of fish are gone. The big ones have disappeared. Now I use a very small gauge net to drag for fish and still don't get many. It takes longer and I catch less. Sometimes I'm out from evening to morning—not even sleeping—and I just catch fifty-thousand-riel worth."

He gestures at everything he owns—yards of knotted nylon netting and hundreds of elegant wire shrimp traps, batteries and bikes, an old wood house perched solidly on broad stilts.

"If I sold all this stuff, I'd get just a little bit of money—land is expensive so it's not enough. I dream of getting $10,000. If I had that much money I would just dig and build a fish farm. If I could afford for my son to go to school, it would be better."

"There's too many fishermen," explains Sy's wife, Phon Sar. Yards of fishing net sit in soft piles before her; Sar's thin fingers skim across the holes, searching for rips. "Since I was seven or eight years old, the Tonle Sap has been changing a lot. The kinds of fish I knew when I was young have all disappeared." Sar points to the river running behind the house. The level has dipped to muddy creek; a few fishermen carefully push their way out toward the lake. It takes much more net, an impossible length, it seems, to pull the same number of fish from the lake. "When I was five, I could fish right here, but I can't anymore. It's not easy to even access the lake because some parts of the river are completely dry."

The proximity to roads and cities is starting to drain one population from this overcrowded village. The teenagers are leaving "because they cannot fish," says Sar. "My niece and nephew just went to Siem Reap to work."

At the edge of Kampong Luong floating village, where the lake melts into the horizon, I stop and watch a pair of fishers. The women mirror one another from the two ends of their boat: moon-faced Ay Srok and her thirty-two-year-old daughter Jom Sreymom. Legs folded under her, egret-like, Srok perches at the bow, spooling out yard after yard of fishing net. Srok wears a broad gingham hat covered with cartoon sheep that have faded in the sun. Her daughter sports flowered pants. Their movements are easy, mechanical even, a dance they've been perfecting since Sreymom was a child. It is just after dawn and the sun slices up from the lake, rose clouds stretching long and low.

Today, they're fishing trey riel. With quick fingers, mother and daughter pull out each tangled fish and flip it into the hull. Their boat is the slim turquoise type. It sits heavy in the lake and is made of wood worried soft by years of water and feet. We're told it's leaky, no good for venturing out much farther than the edges of Kampong Luong—certainly no good for taking deeper into the Tonle Sap, where the wind has lately been pummeling boats much larger than theirs and sending the fish hiding.

There used to be better fishing in this spot, but most of the fish are gone. If the pair caught ten pounds before, that was a decent morning this time of year. Now, they're lucky to catch half. The wind, too, is making it harder not just to fish but to live. The same night Hien and his family jumped into the water to buttress their home, this mother and daughter had to decamp to a neighbor's larger houseboat—it was too dangerous for them to stay put.

Through some miracle of thrift, the women have been able to save enough to buy a small plot of land in Krakor. The land is three hundred square feet and sits just a mile from the market. It cost $1,900, they tell me with the faintest hint of pride.

"Many people want to move to the mainland, but they have no money. For us, we saved for a long time," Sreymom says.

I ask how she feels about moving—leaving the only life she has known. Sreymom brushes off such heavy-handed takes on this decision. This is practical and good; to even be able to consider such a change places them among the fortunate.

"We can't say we're happy to move, but it's difficult to stay. Our home is here, but we can't work here, so our young people have to move," she says.

Her mother interjects.

"I lived here, my parents lived here, my child, from generation to generation," Srok says quietly.

7 *Spare Yourself One Hundred Days of Tears*

On the banks of the Kampong Luong inlet, there's an unsettling new ritual. Each evening, it seems, a family from one of the nearby floating villages draws up in a boat piled high with their worldly belongings. The fan. The blankets. The empty jerry can and plastic flowers and money box and shrine. All of it is pulled off the boat and hauled onto a waiting flatbed truck. When the boat is finally empty, that goes in too— maneuvered up the shore and heaved along the length of the truck by half-a-dozen men, coming to rest on top of the other possessions. By the time the workers finish lashing it to the bed, they've created some mythical beast: half-truck, half-boat, the prow extending past the cab, pointing up at the now-darkened sky.

Tonight, a woman and her children are getting ready to depart. They clutch pillows and twist at bag handles as they watch the men slowly turn their watercraft into a land one. When everything has been loaded up, the family will crowd into the cab and drive twelve hours to Vietnam. At forty-five, Mai hasn't been back in twenty years. Her children, all born and raised in Cambodia, have never set foot in their mother's country.

"We can't get by here because there's no fish," Mai explains, keeping one eye on the truck. Her purse is strapped crosswise to her chest, a back-pack and small cooler rest at her feet. A daughter hugs a zipped square of hammock, her younger brother hovering by her side. They stand, silently, with the rest of the onlookers who have gathered for the spectacle.

"Business is so bad, we can't make enough to eat," Mai says, pushing at the hair frizzing out from her crown. "I have six kids and there's nothing to eat here so we have to go back to Vietnam. No one has any money, so we have to go back."

The family has decided that Mai's mother and one daughter will stay. They'll remain on the lake, looking after their home, in the hopes that the situation will improve and the others can return. Some neighbors have just been wholly moving out. The ethnic Vietnamese villages are emptying: one abandoned home after another left bobbing on the water.

"In five days, five families have left," a bystander tells me. "It's getting hard to make a living here. Fisheries officials are really cracking down and arresting everyone. You have to pay one million or two million riel to get out. I got arrested and had to pay 1.2 million riel to get out. They're always arresting people."

Some watching, though, are likely to be muttering under their breath: "good riddance."

Ask any Khmer fisher about what's happened to the Tonle Sap and the word *yuon* will almost certainly float into the many explanations. Yuon is slang for Vietnamese; it is the most commonplace of words but can also be deeply derogatory. Whether they're using it as a cruel slur or as a casual descriptor stripped of rancor, the fishers are adamant the Vietnamese are the problem. There are too many Vietnamese on the lake; there are too many fishing with illegal methods; there are too many bribing officials and working in cahoots, speeding out to the center of the lake to take the big fish. "Over there is the Vietnamese village," my boat driver once pointed out as we sped past. "And there is the Cambodian. They're separate. We're going to have a war soon," he said, laughing.

The reality is far more complex. If some of the biggest illegal trawlers are operated by Vietnamese, plenty are operated by Khmer—and all are doing so with some Cambodian authority's collusion. Meanwhile, the ethnic Vietnamese population as a whole is the poorest and most vulnerable among Cambodia's fishing communities.

This group is the handiest of scapegoats; the hatred a flashpoint that even today occasionally sparks into violence. Significant territory lost to Vietnam since the 1600s, French preference for importing Vietnamese workers and civil servants during its administration, badly drawn colonial maps, and a decade of Vietnamese occupation following the fall of the Khmer Rouge have all contributed to deep animosity. When it peaks, hostility transforms into terrorism. Hundreds of thousands of ethnic Vietnamese were driven from Cambodia during the Lon Nol regime in the 1970s in pogroms that killed thousands. Once the Khmer Rouge took over, the targeted attacks continued, sending ethnic Vietnamese fleeing into neighboring Vietnam. Those who stayed faced genocide—marked as a foreign enemy. Still, after the fall of the Khmer Rouge, most returned to the only home they had ever known: Cambodia's waterways.[1]

For many, however, documentation that might have proven their Cambodian residency or citizenship was lost in the chaos of war. Without papers, the water is where most of Cambodia's ethnic Vietnamese have remained—a floating, stateless community numbering perhaps 700,000 of the country's roughly 16.5 million population. Even among those whose parents, grandparents, great-grandparents, and ancestors further back were born in Cambodia, most have found it impossible to obtain identification documents. Without those, there can be no school, no government healthcare, no chance of obtaining a land title. And so most of them stay on the water, eking out the exact same living in the exact same place as their ancestors have for centuries, be it a weak echo of what it once was.

"During the fall of the water level we see boats of all sizes sent from Cochinchina to the Great Lake of miraculous fishing," the French lieutenant Jules Marcel Brossard de Corbigny recounted. The river reversal "is the life of the fishermen that Spring brings there each year, and the most extensive source of trade among the races of Indochina."[2]

The Annamites from Cochinchina, as the colonial French termed the South Vietnamese and their country, didn't just enter the Tonle Sap with the yearly floods—they lived there. Henri Mouhot, the explorer, wrote of "a floating population of Annamites,"[3] and a young member of a colonial expedition named Louis de Carné detailed their life on the lake: "The Anna-mites give themselves almost wholly to their fisheries. Some thousands of their boats are employed on the lake itself, and in the arm which connects it with the Mekong, and loaded very deep with the fish taken," he wrote. "Vil-lages are scattered thinly along the banks, others come out over the water, the frail posts which support the huts bending under the force of the waves without its seeming to trouble the inmates. They are Annamites, and, like the buffalo, their faithful servant, if the land fails them, they take to the water."[4]

Ice comes to the lake in the early morning, from a truck packed with sky blue rectangles taller than a child. The blocks have their own atmosphere, swirling clouds across their handlers. One man swings a pick at a block, catches at its center, and slides it onto a waiting platform. With five quick moves, another man saws the ice in half and pushes it toward a waiting boat. Along its route, the ice will be divided and divided yet again: planks for coolers, chunks for beer, slivers for coffee. Split ever smaller as the day wears on and all the while melting back into the Tonle Sap.

Boats crowd in here, at the edge of the inlet leading to Kampong Luong and the smaller floating villages. They are parked two deep at the mucked bank where land meets water—the vendors beginning their brisk trade with the middlemen. Loads are divvied up and transferred from motorbikes and trucks to boats. A pig head tilts at the sky, sniffing air through bloodless nostrils. Green mangoes—firm and sour—are humped up in a bow. Bitter melon stretches the skin of a plastic bag. Fish, fat snakeheads straight from the farm, are coiled into a wicker basket.

A vendor in a Barbie-pink sweater and matching sandals drags an enormous basket of lettuce onto her wooden rowboat. A trio of sellers sit in their boats, the metal bowls of their scales collecting the rising sun. One kneels in front of a mound of thin eggplants, arranging them on a tarp; a neighbor settles herself before her cutting boards; a third readies to push off with her herbs.

This group rents their boats, $10 for each day, and then there's the outlay for the food. Selling to people who have no other way to get vegetables, eggs, or snacks should be easy enough, but the economics of the lake just aren't working anymore. More and more frequently the vendors are falling into debt themselves, spending more than they earn.

"I don't know what to do or how to make a living, I just go day by day. I've done this for twenty years and this is the worst year," one of the vendors tells me in 2016. A wild, flower-patterned hat screens her face and her plaid shirtsleeves are rolled down to the wrist against the sun. She sells chicken and palm sugar, things a family might be willing to forego. If they're even there to sell to anymore.

"Business is very difficult compared with before. Most of the Vietnamese went home to their country. They can't make a living from fishing. The government arrests them, and they just go back to their country," the vendor continues. "Generally, everyone has it so difficult. In the village they can't find anything to eat. When you drive the boat you'll see some houses with no people—the Vietnamese went back to Vietnam. And the Cambodians, some have gone to Thailand."

She begs off and pushes out. A few minutes later, we follow, carving up the gray-green inlet toward the floating homes. By the time we get to the lake's edge, morning has fully broken, and the sky is streaked hot blue and white, spilling silver atop the brown orbit of the Tonle Sap. As he slices forward, Seng Sokum, our skipper, looks toward villages in the distance, squinting out from under his cap. He's dressed for business in his polo shirt and khakis, a gleaming new phone bulging his pocket, edging out toward the small tear in his seam. A steering pole extends from the outboard engine, and Sokum keeps his hand curled around it, a gentle push directing the propeller. He's kicked off his sandals and leans, perched against the small stool at the stern, one bare foot keeping balance on the hull.

The villages here are numbered. Sokum points them out for us: villages 1, 2, 3, and 5 are ethnic Vietnamese, maybe twelve hundred families in total. They've been moving out, he says, leaving behind their sparse floating homes. The Cambodians, too, are moving off the lake that can no longer support them.

Before he got this rental boat, Sokum worked as a fisherman, like his father before him. He hopes his three-month-old son can grow up to have a good job, something far off the lake.

"In the future, poor people will become slaves for rich people because they can't support themselves," he says with a wry laugh. "If the government created opportunities for people, created investment, Cambodians would not have to leave."

Upending history, it now goes like this: the water failing them, they take to the land.

It's early morning at a port near the bottom of the lake and the cockle boats are being emptied at a clip. A teen digs at the shrinking mound of shells—thumbnail-sized mollusks heaped up in the hull like gravel. He's using a plastic jerry can with the top corner sawed off for easy scooping; each pour into the waiting hamper sounds like a hailstorm. The boy fills the basket to its brim with cockles and a skinny kid in a Hollister hoodie and acid-washed jeans grabs at it like it's nothing, like it's not thirty pounds or more, and empties it into a waiting polypropylene sack. The team moves fast, crunch and scoop and pour while their boss, a woman wearing hot pink pants rolled to the knees and a fat clutch of bracelets round her wrist, holds the bags steady. When a bag is full, upwards of one hundred pounds, she swiftly sews the top closed with a length of red plastic string. One, two, three, four, five. The bags are piling up faster than the laborers can move them, sweat trailing down their necks as they heave each sack one by one onto a waiting flatbed truck. All around the workers, a fine dusting of shells lies lightly on the red dirt like prehistoric snow.

There is no large-scale government policy to move people off the water, but across the lake, in various individual communities, officials appear to be toying with such an idea. Thinny Sothy, the deputy chief of the Fisheries Administration's Siem Reap cantonment, says he'd like to move the fishers to land and teach them a different trade. "Our strategy is to encourage them to do another business while fishing. It's more sustainable and will help them live better."

Sothy is a young guy, tubby as befits his status, dressed in a clean khaki uniform. He gesticulates as he speaks, and a silver snake wound round his finger throws the light with each point. We meet him in a shack-like station, at the back of a market not far from where tourist boats set off to visit the floating villages.

Sothy lists the problems facing the lake and its people. His men drift into the office and listen politely.

"Climate change—this is the big problem, and especially dams on the upper level. Fish normally breed up there, the dams block water and they can't migrate. Cambodian people, they depend on the fish in the Tonle Sap. In the past only one million people lived around the lake, now there's six million."

Sothy's remit covers almost half the lake and, while he's loath to address questions around large-scale illegal fishing or corruption, downplaying their impact, he admits the current situation on the lake is barely sustainable.

"I'm also concerned about the lake supporting the people," he says.

In some areas, charities have taken on the work of the government, though with mixed results. Cambodia abounds with nonprofits; thousands are registered, ranging from tiny community initiatives to enormous multinational nongovernmental organizations, to say nothing of the numerous foreign aid agencies and development banks.

Like everything, these come with their own set of problems: some fall prey to corruption and embezzlement, others lie to spur fundraising, the worst perpetuate gross abuses of their own. And then, even in the best of circumstances, there is the question of how their activity unbalances the obligations of government.[5] Still, they fill a desperate need, stepping in with rice or medication, scant schooling, or housing, when it seems no one else will.

Just off National Road 63, partway between Siem Reap city and the lake's northern rim, a little-visited ninth-century Angkorian temple called Prasat Phnom Krom sits on a small hill. A few hundred yards on toward the lake, dirt roads meander west from the graveled two-lane highway, spilling into grasslands and golden paddy fields. The houses at the edge of this land sit in the shadow of Phnom Krom and cut an odd sight: they stand in two rows, identical blonde wood boxes topped with sky-blue roofs. They're large and cookie-cutter, so out of place next to the modest, varied neighboring homes that come in all shades and heights and are patched with every conceivable material. Some unknown nonprofit bought the land and built these uncanny houses, selling them at a low cost to a lucky few before vanishing into the ether, leaving residents to buy and sell as they pleased.

Sles El, Aiy Sash, and their four children ranging in age from two to fourteen are among the newest residents—eight months, now, on land. The family purchased the home from a neighbor and moved off their houseboat, one less thing to worry about as the fishing worsened.

Up close, the houses lose their grace. The new wood is warping, bloating until windows and doors become trapped in their frames—there's a reason most homes here have metal walls and shutters that drop down on a hinge. But land is land, and the family is relieved to have left the water.

"I was a fisherman since I was young, and I lived on the water since I was young. I just moved to land now for the first time," says El, who is thirty-six. "I think living on the mainland is much easier."

School is close by, and there's no worry of his youngest children falling into the lake. The fishing has become untenable. And, posing danger for a small boat, the winds have been worsening each year due, in part, to the mass deforestation birthing new land like his.

"Now you can see, there is a bit of forest but in front there is rice," he says, gesturing at the paddy abutting a hill all but stripped of its trees. "In rainy season, you can't even find a tree to tie your boat to."

As El speaks, his two small sons play on a motorbike behind him, while their older sister looks on. He glances at his children and gathers his thoughts.

"I don't want my kids to follow me to become fishermen. It's hard work, you don't sleep well. I just hope they can get a different job."

It's late afternoon and Reth Roth is nudging her adult son awake, shaking at his shoulder. "It's time to get up," she yells in his ear. Her husband, Cheng Chak, is already dressed, gathering together phones, cigarettes, a camp stove. Their son sleeps like a dead man, unmoving, and then, suddenly, he is up. Sun is streaming through the open sides of the house, sliding along the spacious, bare floors. He blinks, confused, and moves to grab supplies.

Ten minutes later, twenty feet below, the men are loading up a minute wooden boat. There is gas, water, nets, and a cooler. Roth runs down with a handful of instant coffee packets: fuel to make it to dawn. It's early December, just a month into dry season, but, already, the water has dropped far below the house. Father and son will push out past tangled mangroves and clumps of trash, making their way through the narrow waterways into the Tonle Sap. And then, like they do every night, they will fish.

The fishing, at this moment in 2017, is decent. It is the height of the season, which means they can net up to ninety pounds a trip, says Roth. If they compare it to last year, when there was a drought, or the year before, when there was another drought, the fishing is better. If they compare it to "before," however, it is much, much worse.

Before, they could catch a fish in the slim inlet behind the houses, just by dropping a line down from their window. Before, they could catch snakehead fish without even trying. Before, Roth says, "this area was all forest." Now, Phnom Krom village is filled with scores, if not hundreds, of houses. More people competing for fewer fish.

Roth's house is surrounded by a sizable square of watery land—but this is an anomaly. Most of the homes nearby are squeezed against one another. Worn wood stilts jut out from concrete foundations. Walkways banded together from scrap wood pass beneath one neighbor's house to the next. When the water recedes, the floodplains pile with rubbish. Many of the houses are minuscule—inventive, ramshackle affairs of thatch and rusted zinc.

Still, this village, located near the northern tip of the lake barely ten miles south of Siem Reap city, represents the top of the hierarchy for Tonle Sap residents.

Roth, Chak, and their five children moved here thirteen years earlier, when the land was cleared by the government and parceled out. The family came from the water, from a crowded floating home that they piloted place to place. Fishing is a bit simpler when you live on the water—you need less gas, you don't travel as far—but in every other way imaginable, "living on the mainland is much easier," says Roth.

They may not have farmland, but anyone living in a stilt village sees at least some of the same chief benefits. On the mainland, you can access schools, markets, and hospitals. If the fishing is bad, you can find other work: Chak drives a tuktuk, Roth cultivates lotus root behind her house and sells it at the market. It's crucial to have other work because it's impossible to live off the fish alone.

"I have to do two businesses," Chak had told me, when we first met in March. "If I'm just fishing, I can't support my family. If I'm just driving the tuktuk, I cannot support them either. When I lived on the water before, there were a lot of fish. Now there's not so much, but two jobs can equal it out."

A niece, Kout Thoeun, visiting for the day from her own floating home, interjected: "If I could move to the land, I would change my business. I don't know what I would do; we're fishers and we marry fishers and stay fishers." But she was certain anything would be an improvement. "I want my daughter to keep studying. I want her to graduate. And I want her to find a different job on the mainland."

Prince Puthisen was born and raised into horror: his mother and eleven aunts had been blinded by the evil Santema, sent to a cave, and forced to eat their newborns. Only Puthisen survived, growing to manhood and promising vengeance for his destroyed family. Through trickery, he came to marry Kong Rei—daughter of his mortal enemy. And she, madly in love, divulged her mother's terrible deeds and told Puthisen how to access magic. The marriage ended in heartbreak. Puthisen set out to recover the stolen eyeballs of his family and enact his revenge. Kong Rei chased him, begging the prince to return to her. Instead, he flooded the land. A lake spread, separating the couple. Kong Rei threw her body upon the ground and cried herself to death. She became a mountain, her back and head nestled into the ground, an arm thrown despairingly forward.

Phnom Kong Rei lies at the southern lip of the Tonle Sap, where it spills into its river. If you sit on the bank and stare at the mountain from the right angle, that is what you will see: the hopeless princess prone on the ground, sprawled before the water that tore away her love.

On a drizzly April afternoon, Ly Oeu sips an iced coffee and considers how his life has changed since he left the water two years earlier. In 2015 he moved with his family and neighbors from a nearby floating village to this dusty, new community on a steep bank near the bottom of the lake. Here, just a few miles outside of Kampong Chhnang city, plots were cheap enough that the fifteen families could just about manage to afford them. The river is only a few hundred yards away, but the ground is so high we can't see it from here. Instead, there's a view of Phnom Kong Rei—the poignant slopes a hazy blue-green in the distance.

Oeu crosses his arms against his crisp, white T-shirt and screws his mouth into a knot while he mulls his two lives.

"Living on a boat is different than living on land. At that time, we had six kids. Sometimes when we slept, my feet would hit my kids' heads. Sometimes, they'd kick mine." Eventually, the family moved to a roomier floating house. The children grew up and left home. But life on the water hardly got easier. "Our living depends on fishing. If we can't fish, it affects our lives."

On the land, Oeu and his wife, Saros, built their house and were done—no need to buy new floats every few years or replace rotting walls. Half of the house serves as a cafe, the only one in the village so far and a growing side business. Folding tables are ranged the dirt floor, topped with porcelain teapots featuring cartoon deer and small sugar bowls. A jumble of electric cords snake from an extension. A large TV, perched on a neatly hewn wood ledge, peers down at customers. The coffee is thick with sugar and a silky dollop of condensed milk.

The group chose this spot because of its proximity to the water; their boats stay moored there and they still fish most days. But land has offered other options too. Or, more accurately, without enough fish to get by on, life has demanded them.

Over the past few years, the children have moved to Phnom Penh to work in garment factories. The money they send home now supports their parents.

"If we just depended on fishing, we wouldn't have enough money," says Oeu.

And so this land, too, is being transformed. By early 2017, the forest that was once here has been completely cut down. A road came in a year earlier. There are dump trucks and bulldozers the day I visit, leveling out a sweeping plain of cleared, dry dirt. It's being readied into parcels—part of a government plan to move hundreds more families off the river.

Saros is skeptical that this alone will save the fish. "It's difficult to say that moving people will make a difference. Unless illegal equipment declines, the fishing won't improve."

And so the newcomers, too, will find they need much more. They'll need money for their electricity and water; money for gas to get to markets; money to make payments on the loans they'll likely have to take on their land and homes. They'll need to find second jobs, a new way of living. Their kids will need to leave for the factories, the construction sites. Even now, despite all the trappings of a step up, "it's very difficult," admits Oeu. "We live hand to mouth."

8 *Frogs Get Lost in Lakes*

When Vien Ny was a boy, the inlet behind his Kampong Khleang house "was a fresh, blue color." He gestures at the water as he speaks—it is a rich, milky brown, with oily suds floating on its surface. "Lots of things are changing here."

Ny is dressed in camouflage pants and a faded black shirt. An army hat with a gold-thread insignia sits sharp on his crown. Many years ago, Ny was a soldier. But he's been a fisherman for more than a decade now, raising his family just a few miles away from where he grew up.

Ny drags on a cigarette as he details the differences. The water is low, there's no forest, the climate is changing, and the teenagers in the area seem to fight constantly. The fish are just gone. Three years back, Ny decided to switch to shrimping instead. The traps are footlong wire-and-mesh affairs priced about $1 a piece. Shrimpers buy them by the hundreds. They wear out quickly, but they do the job. In the high season, Ny sets scores of his shrimp traps along the turbid inlets and makes around $4 a day, after expenses.

By the end of dry season, however, Ny can catch only about fifty cents worth of shrimp each day. So it's manual labor instead: carrying heavy bags of cockles up at the port.

"This season we don't have enough to buy food. If I work, it's okay. If I can't, I borrow money from neighbors and pay them back in the wet season."

The youngest of Ny's children and a grandchild run in loops behind him, climbing on and off his motorbike, clambering under his legs.

"I can't predict their future, but I think I want them to find other jobs," Ny says. Catching fish is simply the work done by someone with no farmland, education, or other options. "We are poor and can't send them to school, we need them to work. When we don't know any other job, what else can we do? This is why we are fishermen."

Ny talks with us until it's time for him to gently shoo the children off his moto and head to the pagoda. He's hoping to get his arm blessed after hurting it while hauling hundred-pound loads. A visit to the clinic is too expensive so a prayer must suffice.

Luon Thear, Ny's twenty-year-old daughter drifts over. She has a three-year old and a two-year old and is pregnant with her third child. Her young family catches shrimp, too. Every day Thear's husband sets two hundred to three hundred traps. They earn a few dollars a day and can support themselves, just about, with that. But they can't save. If there's an injury, if someone gets sick, if the traps get stolen, there's no room for maneuvering. Today, her husband, the fisherman, is out working as a laborer like his father-in-law.

It's not ideal. With day labor, you take the job when you can get it, she explains; there isn't work all the time. Fishing brings in something every day; or it should, anyway.

The road leading toward Kampong Luong floating village is a faded orange that darkens where its banks spill into the water, coloring it the same burnished shade as the cloudy river. The houses here are set on dusty ground, too fragile to sit in the water permanently. Their stilts are just a foot or so tall: thin legs holding up four walls of plywood, tarp, and cardboard. There's a small market, collaged out of dozens of pieces of wall and roof: red and green layered thickly against one another. Old house boats, bleached in the sun, sit marooned on the grass: a pale, expansive prairie stretching out toward the lake.

This is where Phan Srey's home is set in the dry season. The house is one wood room on hard packed soil, small enough and light enough to be pulled by motor-cart to higher banks when the rains begin to fall. Srey is a charcoal seller who works the lake, moving through Kampong Luong and the smaller villages by hired boat. Now, it's so dry, "I can't even row the boat."

While Srey speaks, she pulls at her ponytail. It's early in the day, but already she is drained and stressed.

"It's difficult because the water is too low. The fishermen can't make money from fishing so businesspeople can't make money either," she says.

This year, Srey has ducks. They're long-necked and dirty, quacking from inside the confines of their bamboo cage. It's a stab at a second business—sell the eggs, sell the ducks—but so far, they've just cost money and earned her nothing. Worse, some have already died from the heat.

The only way to get a reliable income involves leaving, she tells me. "Here, hundreds of families go to Thailand to work." While Srey speaks, her twelve-year-old son stalks a chicken across the yard and readies it for butchering. He left school months earlier—his mother needs the help at home. More than that, there simply isn't enough money to keep him enrolled.

Srey's older children have scattered. One lives in Battambang, another in Phnom Penh, a third went to a factory in Thailand just last week. From there, they can send a little bit of cash back to their widowed mother. It's barely enough to live off of; but there's no chance they could earn anything from the lake.

"They don't want to stay here, they want to go somewhere else."

Teenage sons and daughters are leaving the lake in droves, seeking city work with the rest of Cambodia's rural children. For some, these changes are welcome. Life outside the village can bring anonymity and experience: new relationships, new things to learn about, new ways to view the world. The lucky ones thrive when they move away. They find work on a well-run construction site, at a model factory, in a good security firm. The hours are long, but manageable, and the pay is decent; maybe there is even a chance to move up in the ranks. Back home, their families prosper. The houses grow nicer; wood is swapped for concrete. A shiny new Scoopy motorbike, its engine purring, takes the place of a mangled Daelim.

But successes like these are few and far between. Far more often, the kids who leave end up on subsistence wages. There's little time or money for friends, classes, or any color to one's life. Instead, the sons and daughters move away only to find a new kind of scratched survival.

As villages bleed out their youth, Cambodia has grown more reliant on remittances. In 2019 some $2.8 billion—more than 10 percent of that year's GDP—was sent in by overseas workers.[1] Though it is harder to calculate, an immense amount of money is sent by internal migrants, those who leave home to be security guards and waitresses, salespeople and sex workers, and, above all, garment workers and construction laborers.

The roads snaking out from every city in Cambodia are lined with factories: in total, more than a thousand squat, hangar-like buildings sit behind dull concrete fences. Cambodian factories produce bikes and circuit boards and aluminum coils, but garment manufacturing—from high-end designer clothing down to the cheapest fast fashion—forms the foundation of the economy. Some seven hundred fifty thousand people, mostly women, work at these garment factories—long days in badly ventilated rooms. Garment workers regularly skip off-days for overtime as this is the only way, really, to earn enough to cover the cost of living. With overtime, the average monthly salary is $200. Most of that is spent on renting small, airless rooms and paying for the commute, which entails traveling to and from work in tightly packed trucks that crash not infrequently and sometimes fatally. If a few dollars can be scraped together after all these costs, workers send them home. Often, they do so at the expense of their own meals.

The multiplying factories mimic the rest of Cambodia's urban development. In all these cities, umpteen buildings are under construction: skyscrapers, townhouses, supermarkets, luxury villas, suburban cul-de-sacs, and office towers. This is where the rest of the workers go. There are an estimated two hundred thousand laborers, mostly men, employed in an almost entirely unregulated sector, where the pay rarely tops $10 a day. Construction workers sleep onsite to save money and work in flip-flops.

Injuries, even death, are commonplace. And though many leave home for these jobs intending to earn money to send back to their families, most construction workers, like the garment workers, find they can barely cover their own daily needs.

To earn anything worthwhile, then, it is necessary to go abroad. This comes with its own set of struggles. While there are a handful of formalized, well-paying programs—such as those run by South Korea—most overseas jobs in Thailand, Malaysia, and farther afield are arranged informally through brokers and come with certain risks. It is not uncommon for workers to return with no money after bosses withhold wages entirely. The most unfortunate end up in truly dire situations. Women leave to work as housekeepers, only to be raped and starved by their employers. Men leave for farm work, only to be trafficked onto fishing boats where they are enslaved and tortured. The stories circulate on local radio and Facebook, through public service announcements, murmured among neighbors. Few would-be migrant workers are totally ignorant of the risks of leaving, but still the villages empty out. There are no other options.

Chet Krel was raised in a fishing family. He's seventeen now, track pants and hair combed forward like a K-pop star. To make ends meet, Krel works as a laborer. It's just day labor, carting cement, hauling bricks. All he wants is to be a fisherman and he fears, deeply, having to leave Kampong Khleang.

"I need to get another job, but I think fishing is much better than construction. I listen to the radio, and they broadcast these reports: some workers are shot by their managers. They run away. They don't get paid." Fishing is simple. "I catch fish, I sell it, I make money."

A large houseboat is moored at the muddy inlet to Kampong Luong, three inches of water lapping garbage against its hull. Blue paint chips off the walls, a TV antenna and small solar panel unfurls from the rusted aluminum roof. Faded clothes are drying below its overhang. A few potted plants, their green sharp against the graying wood, blaze in the setting sun.

Lay Vinn lives here with his wife, pregnant daughter, and son-in-law. He works as a tourist boat driver, ferrying Cambodian and foreign visitors through the winding canals of the nearby floating villages—though the dropping water means fewer tourists than ever. His wife sells vegetables on the waterways. His children "all want to live somewhere else."

The son-in-law, Sok Lan, crosses the border regularly. He's worked on Thai fishing boats and as a hired laborer on Thailand's industrial-scale farms. If his wife weren't about to give birth, Lan says, he would leave immediately.

"There's nothing here, there's no work. Here, I just do some small jobs carrying vegetables or clams," he says. "I want to go work in another country."

On the banks of Kok Ai, the small patch of disappearing land where the Tonle Sap spills into Battambang's Sangke River, Mat Min and his two sons stand in the water pulling at a net. The catch is dismal. "I think if the government was strict about the fishing laws, maybe in the future there would be a lot of fish," one son says hopefully. The other, Shavi, picks small fish from the net, tossing them into a nearby basket. Shavi spent more than a year working in Thailand, only to be cheated out of his pay. "I only got enough money for my transportation. I don't want to go back."

While in Thailand, Shavi was arrested, along with fifty other undocumented migrant workers, his father tells me. They were detained for eight months and then deported: just one more group of workers returning home without anything to show for it. And now, in 2017, Shavi is back on the Tonle Sap, trying to catch fish in these same barren waters. "I'm not sure what I'll do in the future," he says. "Now, I'm just fishing."

The children of the Tonle Sap aren't leaving only because of the worsening catch and failing business. They're leaving because family debt here, as everywhere in the country, has become so unmanageable. About a quarter of Cambodian adults have a microfinance loan and the average debt owed by each borrower is around $3,300—the highest in the world, and more than twice the GDP per capita.[2]

Before the government capped interest rates on microfinance loans at 18 percent in 2017, interest could reach as much as 50 percent.[3] Today, though, there are still few rules on fees or loan size. Countless Cambodians have had their land seized for nonpayment, with researchers estimating that as much as 15 percent of rural land has been lost in this manner.[4] On the lake, the situation is no different. Everyone owes money: even those without a patch of land to sink their stilts into, even those with just a boat to their name.

These loans are impossible to keep up with. Double debt or even triple debt is not uncommon, with fishers borrowing from neighbors at even higher interest rates so as not to fall back on their bank repayments. On every factory floor, on every building site, there is a direct through line back to this debt.

"Only the very poorest" have no slaves at all, Zhou Daguan observed during his travels around the city of Angkor. Families often had a hundred or more. The poorer among them had at least "ten or twenty." Zhou outlined the value and prices of the enslaved. When they ran away and were caught, they "must carry a dark blue tattoo on their face, and sometimes an iron shackle around their neck or between their arms and legs."[5]

Among those enslaved people were no small number of "debt slaves"—those forced into servitude to repay a loan. This practice continued through the twentieth century. Today, debt bondage persists in particular industries, like brick making—where parents and even their young children labor in dangerous kilns to pay off loans made by the factory owners. Those who seek work abroad through a broker sometimes land in the same arrangement, paying off the costs fronted for their travel expenses and job placement. But even those not enslaved are invariably bonded in no small way by their debt. In theory, they can obtain freedom through work. But the terms change. There is no way to escape.

Debt may look different now, but from the Angkorian empire through colonial rule on forward, it has long placed an impossible weight upon the farmer and fisher. The French, who administered the country from 1863 to 1953, levied extraordinarily steep taxes—the highest rates within their

Indochina empire.[6] Those who could not pay labored forcibly, perhaps as much as ninety days a year.[7] In northwestern Cambodia, those living under Siamese rule, which held power over substantial portions of the country from the late eighteenth to early twentieth centuries, fell prey to a similar system. Every citizen "had to pay one baht, one samlueng, and one luang" to their village head, Adolf Bastian, a German ethnographer, meticulously outlined in 1864.[8] This was used to purchase spices and beeswax to send "as tribute" to Bangkok. If those tributes went up in price, so too the individual burden, which quickly bore down. In the same decade, Henri Mouhot wrote about an acquaintance he made in Siam, who hoped to travel with him to Cambodia.[9] The man was deep in debt, "badly off." Mouhot added up the farmer's many obligations, thirty-nine ticals in all, he calculated. "His land brings him in forty after all expenses are paid; what can he do with the one remaining tical?"

Always, debt plagues; chipping away until no options remain.

Keo Sina is thirty-two and would like to get married. Instead, he lives with his parents and some of his nine sisters and brothers—a revolving door of young men and women trying, and failing, to support their parents and build up their own lives. In this family, the children are studious: they learn languages and enroll in classes. Then, invariably, one must quit school to work and keep a younger sibling studying. Two sisters work in Siem Reap city, one works in Phnom Penh. The brothers come and go. They work in factories and restaurants, construction and small businesses—and nothing they do seems to get them ahead.

The family home is a dizzyingly high stilted house in the center of Kampong Khleang village. During the wet season, the lake swells to lap at their porch. Now, in May 2016, steep wood planks serve as a stairway thirty feet down to hard packed dirt. Each month, money comes in from the children: $20 here, $30 there. It does not add up to much.

"Just this year some of our kids and neighbors went to work as construction workers. They make $100 a month, and it's not enough to pay the bank," says Chum Kear, Sina's sixty-one-year-old father.

Like everyone in this village, the family is deeply in debt. Three years ago, Kear and his wife, Kay Oeun, borrowed $4,000 from a microfinance institution, or MFI, to purchase shrimp traps.

"We borrowed to make a new business, but it isn't working," he explains. "I can't make money at all, and I owe the bank a lot."

Among his neighbors, says Kear, this is common. "Some people who live here don't have enough to eat; many owe money to the MFI."

The family is expected to pay about $200 each month for two long years. With the drought, it's become all but impossible to pay off such loans.

A while back, Sina went to Phnom Penh. He found a job as a security guard, only to get fired a few months later after failing to stop a theft. Now, he travels from his parent's home to Siem Reap city, staying a few days at a time and working as a day laborer. In his spare time, he and his twenty-five-year-old brother fish what they can from the shriveled inlet running alongside the village and out toward the lake.

"I have to support my parents," Sina explains. He's just returned from fishing—a poor show—and has ducked inside to comb his hair and wrap a fresh krama around his waist. "I don't want to go anywhere else. I don't want to go work in Thailand. My friends mostly want to stay here too," he adds.

"My son dreams of buying a plot of land, but it costs a lot of money," his mother explains. "There's no hope on the lake because there's no fish."

"Thus we traversed the beautiful plains, which, when I formerly travelled this road, were inhabited by the poor Thiâmes; but now, in place of rich harvest, I was astonished to find nothing but large trees: the villages were abandoned, and the houses and enclosures in ruins," Henri Mouhot wrote of a struggling Cambodian village in 1860. There, the people suffered not from their debt or the taxes, but simply from gross abuse. These were the sorts of excesses that French colonialism, then in its earliest days, would end up wreaking on the peasantry in the decades to come. Under the Khmer Rouge, such scenes would play out once again. One hundred and fifty years on, mismanagement and corruption take a similar toll today.

In the village Mouhot visited, a local ruler, "executing or exceeding the orders of his master the king of Cambodia, had kept these unfortunate people in such a state of slavery and oppression that they had even been deprived of their fishing and agricultural implements, and being left without money or resources, experienced such frightful poverty that many of them died of hunger."[10]

All around the Tonle Sap, more debt. At the house across from Sina's, Roan Sy borrowed $4,000 to replace stolen nets. Next door, Sao Sok borrowed $4,000 to buy shrimping equipment and a new boat. "A lot of people who live in this area are in a really bad situation. They've all borrowed money from organizations, from banks, from MFIS. All of us have borrowed money."

Inside the sturdy stilted wood homes, inside the crumbling, moveable shacks, inside the floating barges and flooding houseboats: debt.

In Phnom Krom, Reth Roth and her husband, Cheng Chak, have spent a year paying back a $2,000 loan to build their house, with a year left to go. Each month they pay $100 to $125. When their daughter got sick and they needed $40 for her treatment, they turned to a neighboring money lender. Every day, for eighteen days, they will give him $2.50. "If you need money urgently, you can't get a bank loan," explains Roth.

Down the road, Sles El still owes the bulk of the $2,000 he borrowed to purchase their new home. Every month, for two years, he will pay $117.50. "Sometimes, if I don't have enough to pay it back, I borrow from a neighbor."

Off National Road 54, Sok Py, the fish farmer, pays $125 a month on his $2,500 loan. "I borrow money from the bank, but I haven't made much profit. Now I have to borrow money from others."

Ly Oeu's Kampong Chhnang cafe came from a microfinance loan: the land, the coffee, the chairs, the table. "I owe a lot to the MFI. It will be a good business when a lot of people move here, but we don't have the capital." Every month, his children send money back from Phnom Penh, where they work in garment factories. "If we just depended on fishing, there wouldn't be enough money to support the family."

In Kampong Prek, Mok Hien has yet to repay half of a $250 loan. He used the money to repair his boat, to buy new fishing equipment, and replace stolen nets. In years past, Hien would regularly borrow $500 to purchase new nets or carry out necessary repairs—something he could earn back in a matter of months. Now, in 2016, he's borrowed far less but five months on is still struggling to settle up.

He sweeps a hand out toward the floating houses that make up this village. "All of the villagers here have to borrow money." His own family owes money to the bank and to two separate neighbors. He points at a house, a metal shack, which belongs to the money lender. "Some people are really clever," Hien says, almost admiringly. "They borrow from the bank and then loan to the neighbors to get more interest."

To pay, or to try to pay, families must split apart. "I have four children and sixteen grandkids. Some have left, they have their own families. No one goes to Thailand, but they go to Battambang and Phnom Penh."

While Hien talks, the tide pulls out and out. By the time we leave his house in the late afternoon, the water has dipped so low that we must pull the boat to the edge of the village, scraping along pebbles and broken glass, before it's deep enough to drop the long tail motor in.

As we putter back to the land, we pass one boat after another that has paused to lift its propeller from the shallows and disentangle garbage. We reach the inlet leading to the Krakor road, the water frothing gray in our wake. Over the scream of the motor, Hien's words are thrumming in my ears.

"Laos won't open the dam and China won't either and that's why we don't have enough water. There's no jungle anymore, and so there's no rain. Inside the lake there's no big trees left. Inside the forest, there's no big trees. The fish need shelter to stay in. Now, the flooded forest is burning, and the fish have no place to stay—like humans without a roof."

9 *The Gourd Sinks, Broken Glass Floats*

A patch of stunted shrubs, gnarled greenery, peeks above the water. In the distance, there is a line of floating houses, robin egg walls topped with red-rust roofs. Two boats stand here, tiny wood pirogues, bows angled toward one another. A fisher in a bucket hat, his skinny jeans soaked through, lists dangerously as he pulls on his half of the orange net; his striped partner mirrors him from the neighboring boat. The men twist the ends while they pull up the net, a fat hammock of palm-length fish writhing helplessly as water spills from their bodies and back into the lake. A beat later, the fishers have emptied their catch into their boats and moved on to the next doomed expanse.

The lake is full of strange illusions.

During the drought, the Tonle Sap is covered with fine red algae that makes it look as if it's spilling into endless sand flats. The hill-sized Phnom Kong Rei looms in the distance, slim blue humps against the flat belt of the tropical horizon. "Snows crown the peaks, and the sun, which does its best to melt them, without effect, gives them a pale, ethereal look," a nineteenth-century explorer insisted, impossibly.[1] From the sky, one type of fishing trap looks like a massive arrow: an unknown signal. Look out at the lake in one direction and it might be the ocean. Spin around and there are two boats, parked against a bone-dry tree. A man stands nearby, water cutting no higher than his calves.

From Siem Reap to Battambang, a hard surface seems to run the length of the lake bed. "In the middle . . . the remains of an old road had apparently been discovered," Adolf Bastian wrote in 1864.[2] For decades, word of an Angkorian causeway bounced from fisherman to colonialist to researcher—fantastical, improbable, but hunted ceaselessly.[3]

And why shouldn't the impossible be possible here? This is a place where land becomes water, twice each year.

Traveling up a small river leading into the Tonle Sap, I spot smudges on the sky. The boat draws forward and the smudges come undone. They're storks—a cacophony of slender legs and calligraphic wings—folding and unfolding upon one another as they range toward the land.

We pass houses, stilted, then floating, until the inlet spills into a placid sea. The sky is a cloudless, crystalline blue, doubled by the water. The signs of man are like this: A fisherman in a lemon drop T-shirt walks slowly through the water as he spools out a floating net. A woman crouches in her boat, pulling at a trap, her companion standing in the lake, steadying.

Here, the water is just ankle high, where it laps at a sandbar covered in golden bush grass. Two fishers stand threading their net out, out, out. A fishing campsite floats over the lake. It is a tangle of stakes holding up a platform strong enough for four fishers and their hammocks, for coolers, pots, and dozens of traps. Tethered to it are two small boats with motors for daily catch and two big boats with half-moons of tattered tarp for family living. Children wander from the platform to the boats. A TV antenna and a lightbulb are lashed to the tallest stakes.

Let us speak, wrote Lieutenant Jules Marcel Brossard de Corbigny, *of the great lake in the cloudless sky.* This *gigantic heart. The Freshwater Sea*, so abundant that its bounty can be *scooped out by hand*, Zhou Daguan observed. *Talk of tides which can be felt one hundred and seventy leagues* from there; of the *immense sheet as large and full of motion as a sea*; the *dense jungles on the bank*; the *herds of wild elephants*; *trees submerged* to their tops. *Tale Sap, Lake Tale, Thalesab, Touli-Sap, Thala Sap. Tonle Sap.*[4]

In March 2017, a year after the wildfires, Prek Toal is lush again. Upriver, we had boated past low sweeps of land still covered only in the dull brown of dead foliage. But here, it is bright in every direction. Ly Heng leads us behind his home, where a thick carpet of green has overtaken the dark ground. Pale leaves snake across the floor, their vines strangling humps of burned shrubs. The sky is overcast with the promise of a timely rainy season. The water depth is fairly normal. The catch has been much improved. Still, the neighbors stopping by Heng's store don't seem demonstrably better off.

"The fishermen don't have enough money. They ask to pay later all the time. They're still just living hand to mouth. A smart fisherman can make another business and do a bit better. But if they're not smart, it's just hand to mouth."

Heng points out the changes at his own house. He has been installing solar panels—cheaper, over time, than the diesel needed to power his generator. It is an economic consideration, not an environmental one. Despite the slight improvement this year after the drought, the problems on the lake have passed the point of no return.

"I think in the next twenty years, there won't be much change," Heng predicts, "but in fifty or sixty years, things will be very different here."

It strikes me, then, as an optimistic timeline. But even I am taken aback by how fast everything unwinds over the next few years.

In the late 1800s, Louis de Carné, a twenty-three-year-old French diplomat joined several countrymen and a number of locals drafted into servitude on a Mekong expedition through Cambodia, Laos, and China. The Tonle Sap stunned.[5]

"Leaving Compon-Luon, our little gunboat took the direction of the great lake— the Ton-le-sap, a true inland sea, not less than twenty leagues in length when the waters are lowest, but, when the inundation begins, spread over the country till it triples its surface. During the months of August and September there are no roads in the lower districts; boats sail over the fields, trees show their heads above the water, and the wild beasts flee, en masse, to the heights; so that nothing could give a more vivid idea of the deluge," he wrote.

"Presently the wind rises, it blows violently, ploughing deep furrows in the lake. The land is only a blue thread on our right, hardly seen above the waves; on our left the horizon is all sea."

Slowly and then very fast, the seasons stop working. In 2018 there's too much rain and too much water. In July, a dam collapses in Laos, sending its reservoir pouring across the countryside. Whole villages are swept away and scores are killed. The water rushes down the Sekong River across the Cambodian border; thousands hurry to relocate as the river spills its banks, flooding seventeen villages, destroying homes and crops.[6] Already, the Sekong, Sesan, and Srepok, the Mekong and the Tonle Sap had been too full—a tropical storm had sent their levels rising and all of the lower Mekong was struggling with the floods.

A year later, it's gone bone-dry. A drought sweeps the region. In 2019, almost one year to the day after the dam's collapse, the level of the Mekong dips to a record low.[7] An entire dam reservoir in Thailand dries up, revealing the remains of a temple drowned decades earlier.[8] In Laos, less than half the land can be planted on.[9] The Mekong slows to a drip, and so there is no freshwater to push out the salt spilling into Vietnam's delta, destroying crops by the ton.[10]

The Tonle Sap gets one good fishing year, 2018, and then no more. In 2019 the river reverses course months late and that lasts just six weeks—instead of the usual five months. When the lake reaches its maximum volume, it is half the average.[11] In 2020, until a series of brutal flash floods arrive in October, the river never quite reverses course.[12] For nearly the whole wet season, the height of the Tonle Sap stays too low to push any significant amount of water upstream. The volume of the lake reaches just a quarter of its average.[13]

Once again, fishers say the same thing: "We have never seen it like this." "We have never experienced a water level so low." Every year, it seems, there's a new awful superlative to apply to the lake.[14]

Recovery mechanisms have failed completely. In 2017 the fishing came back after the drought year. Debts could be repaid, stocks replenished. In 2020 a fisher might spend an entire day pulling nets and come up with this: a few eels, two snakes.[15] The desperation is growing palpable.

Set at the end of rainy season, Bon Om Touk is a glorious affair. Each November, as the water begins flooding out again from the Tonle Sap, a million Cambodians pack into minivans and buses and head for the capital. This Water Festival, in some iteration or another, is perhaps eight hundred years old. What began as a commemoration of Jayavarman VII's crushing naval defeat of the Chams, morphed, over time, into a thanksgiving of sorts—a celebration of the river's reversal, the fertile pulse.

The nights are for partying. The days are for racing. Spectators throng the riverfront to watch long dragon boats manned by dozens. Two by two, the boats chase down the Tonle Sap River. By then, the water has become dangerous—deep and swift. Branches and tangles of hyacinth unmoored by the swelling river rush alongside the paddlers. Most years, boats overturn. On occasion, racers drown. In 2009 I interviewed a number of captains: their biggest concern, to a man, was the height of the water. They were fishers, they knew how to swim, each assured me, but did I know how they might get lifejackets? "We want to race, to keep our traditions alive—it makes us happy," a rower told me, by way of explaining why he took the risk year after year.

Just a decade later, as their oars rip through the water for the 2019 Water Festival, racers find themselves speeding on a river that has reached a historic low. At the bottom of the concrete quay where the crowds gather, a patch of browning grass stretches out toward the shallow water. The Tonle Sap, lapping at its edges, barely appears to be moving. In 2020 the races are cancelled because of Covid-19: too dangerous to travel, to pack the riverfront, too much poverty streaming across the country.

Then, too, the river never really reverses course—what could there be to celebrate?

It's rainy season, the water halfway up the stairs of Kampong Khleang, and villagers are boating through the river-streets. A woman balances on a wide, wood rowboat, sending her chipped oar cutting through the surface. In the stern, her children arrange the bananas and oil and eggs for sale. Another mother crosses them in a worn pirogue, rowing, squatted on the narrow bow, one eye on the toddler calmly crawling toward her. The water is green-gray, and sunlight spills across the alleys. Farther down the flooded road, a young couple moves an infant off a boat that is pressed against the stairs leading toward their towering home. A man dozes on the deck of his skiff. From one porch, a grandmother and baby peer at the watery scene unfolding below. The light drips golden on the watchers.

Chang Laom rebuilt her life on the Tonle Sap. She was first married during the Khmer Rouge, one of forty-eight couples paired together at the same ceremony, just another among the hundreds of thousands of forced marriages that took place under the regime. She had two sons and a daughter; when their father died, the youngest was just three months old. Laom worked as a housecleaner. She worked in Thailand. And once she finally remarried, she plucked her children from the land and moved them to her new husband's watery home in Prek Toal. After three decades, she is firmly rooted into this world.

"I was scared to live on the water, but I kept trying. If I took a boat, I wouldn't go alone. Even today, I'm still a bit scared," Laom says with a laugh.

A year after the fire, Laom's garden is slowly growing back. She walks us through, once again, pointing out her new crops. In place of charred plants and scrubland, there are now neat rows of pumpkins, melons, and chilies. And yet, nothing is growing quite as it should.

"When you visited last time, my garden was all burned up. Now it's better, but there's still no fruit. You can see: there's flowers and small fruits, but they aren't growing." She points at a stunted pumpkin. Turns and asks if I have any theories.

Laom thinks the fire must have done something to the soil, changed its composition in some manner so that the plants flower but don't bear fruit. It's something beautiful to look at, but it's useless.

ACKNOWLEDGMENTS

First, I must thank every source in this book—gracious with their time and open with their thoughts. I owe an unpayable debt of gratitude to every single person who was willing to speak to me, from the fishermen who shouted out a few words in passing, to the women who welcomed me into their homes, to the officials, academics, and activists who took the time to explain the broader context.

Similarly, I extend a special measure of thanks to Heng Sokharany, Len Leng, Neou Vannarin, and Mech Dara for their translations—with particular gratitude to Chhorn Chansy and Seng Sophea, whose long days on and around the lake formed the bulk of this reporting and whose companionship and insight were incomparable.

The idea for this book would likely never have been sparked if not for Nicolas Axelrod, who thought to document the lake during the 2016 drought and kindly invited me along. When I began writing, I grew ever more grateful for his efforts and photographs, which helped jog my memory and allowed me to add in countless extra detail. Areeya Tivasuradej, who accompanied us on the second trip, offered invaluable insight into the larger regional situation. I am particularly grateful for the map she kept of the trip, which was enormously helpful to my writing.

In addition to his significant support over the years, John Vink was kind enough to invite me along to Kbal Romeas, which helped me to understand the larger geography of Cambodia's dams. I want to thank

Andrea Claassen and her remarkable team for introducing me to Koh Preah and the larger frame of life in the Mekong islands.

A number of researchers offered me their time and insight. Thanks to Ian Baird for walking me through both hydropower damming and the intricacies of fish migration, particularly for his insights into the movement of trey riel. Veronica Walker Vadillo enormously helped inform my understanding of the links between fishing and culture. Thank you to Klairung Amratisha, whose paper on Dik Danle Sap proved a critical introduction to the novel, and who was kind enough to point me to other documentation, even finding and scanning the Sar Kapun poem for me. Brian Eyler has been immensely generous with his time and research over the years and has been paramount to my understanding of the Mekong dam situation. Alison Carter tipped me off to a number of important studies and introduced me to the fascinating work of Voeun Vuthy. When I couldn't find a single copy of George Groslier's book in Phnom Penh, Kent Davis was generous enough to email me chapters of his published translation.

Some of my early reporting on this topic was published in Eater and Devex, and I would like to thank Matt Buchanan and Paul Harris for their significant editorial, logistical, and financial support in shepherding those pieces.

Countless studies, books, and reports also informed this book, and I thank every one of those researchers whom I cited in the endnotes and above. I would like to add additional thanks for work by International Rivers, Melissa Marschke, Brendan M. Buckley, Thol Dina and Jin Sato, Damian Evans, Roland Fletcher, Apisom Intralawan, Matti Kummu, Terry Lustig and Christophe Pottier, Dan Penny, Tyson R. Roberts, Eric Baran, and Nao Thuok, which provided particular inspiration and elucidation.

In addition to providing limitless sage advice, my dear friends Will Baxter, Dene-Hern Chen, Saumya Roy, and Mary Kozlovski read entire drafts, as did my father and my sister Judy, and I am immensely grateful for what proved to be deeply insightful comments and feedback. Special thanks to Dave Boyle, for his feedback on early drafts, and for his years of support during the time I was reporting and conceptualizing this book.

Thanks to David Chandler and Brian Eyler, who reviewed specific chapters and offered expert suggestions. I owe particular thanks to Milton Osborne, who read over a whole draft and made several astute suggestions for expansion, for which I am most grateful. Thanks, too, to Youk Chhang, Sophal Ear, Murray Hiebert, Elizabeth Becker, and Ou Virak for their insightful comments and support during this process.

Robert Carmichael and Sebastian Strangio helped me understand the nuts and bolts of the book writing process and provided ceaseless encouragement over what ended up being a much longer period of time than I anticipated (in spite of Rob's prescient warning years ago to "better make sure you're really engaged with the topic because it will be with it for a long time"). Thanks to Minh Bui Jones, my editor at *Mekong Review*, for championing my work for many years and to Debbie Charles, at Devex, for her wise counsel.

My agent Christopher Rogers at DCL was the first to take a chance on this book, for which I am immensely grateful. Thank you to the entire team at Potomac Books, particularly to my editor Tom Swanson, for his early faith, as well as to Haley Mendlik and Rosemary Sekora and their teams for bringing this book to fruition and for their oversight and patient guidance. Thanks to Irina du Quenoy for her endless, excellent catches in the copyediting stage and extreme patience. And thanks to Taylor Rothgeb for the help throughout.

I owe immense gratitude to every one of my former colleagues at the *Cambodia Daily* and *Phnom Penh Post*, as well as to the larger Phnom Penh and Bangkok communities, whose camaraderie helped me grow as a human and a journalist. Especial thanks are owed to my editors Kevin Doyle and James Welsh for first hiring me and setting me on the right path, and to Chad Williams and Phil Bader for moving me along that road. Though this list is far from comprehensive, in addition to the friends and colleagues listed above, I would like to thank the following folks for helping shape my understanding of Cambodia and providing meaningful support over the years: Alice Foster, Prak Chan Thul, Chhorn Chansy, Charles Fox, Mech Dara, Ellie Dyer, Hayley Welgus, Irwin Loy, Julia Wallace, Kate Bartlett, Len Leng, Michelle Vachon, Kuch Naren, the late Saing Soenthrith, Cheng Sokhorng, Chum Sukim, May Titthara, and Neou Vannarin.

Reporting for this book was helped along by a number of grants, without which I would not have been able to carry out my work. Thank you to the Thomson Reuters Foundation, Stanley Foundation, and Gerda Henkel Stiftung, which invited me to their security workshop and paired me with Areeya—and later gave us a generous grant for visiting the lake, setting me on course for writing this book. I am particularly grateful to Devon Terrill, at Stanley, and Rose Skelton, at TRF, for their support over the following years. The Earth Journalism Network provided helpful funding for my visit to Koh Preah. When I began writing, the Logan Nonfiction Program at the Carey Institute gave me space and freedom to work, along with a dream cohort of fellow writers whom I feel lucky to still call friends. I would like to thank in particular Zan Strumfeld and Josh Friedman, as well as the exceptionally kind and talented Carey Institute staff. A year later, Yaddo invited me to a residency, for which I owe an immense debt of gratitude to their entire staff as well as to the friends I made while there. Being able to experience a new setting and socialize with an exceptional group of artists one year into the pandemic was an unimaginable gift for my mental health and made me more productive than I had been in months.

This book was initially conceived while I was working at Asia Society, and I would like to thank my colleagues there and extend particular gratitude to my bosses at the time, Dan Washburn and Tom Nagorski, who offered a truly rare level of support in allowing me to take time off and work remotely in order to accept the Logan fellowship. I would also like to thank Susie Jakes and the entire ChinaFile team for taking me on at a critical juncture in a way that made it possible for me to finish this book.

I would like to add a particular note of thanks to Sao Sreymom, whose custom map was more beautiful and moving than I ever could have anticipated. Nicolas Axelrod generously provided the Tonle Sap photos inside. I am so grateful for their contributions.

To all my friends in New York, Philadelphia, Washington DC, Chicago, Los Angeles, and abroad, thank you for your incredible friendship and for your kindness during this process and putting up with what must have sounded like a broken record. And thank you to the Weiss, Feinman, and Galin families, for their love and support over the decades.

To my siblings: Judy, Ken, Dean, and Sarah, thank you for being my four lifelong rocks, and thank you for bringing so much more love into my world through Rachel, Susie, Reade, Vicky, Sydney, and Clark, as well as through Joel, Nikki, Racquel, and Matt.

Mom and Dad, I can't tell you how lucky I feel to have parents like you. Your unwavering support over the years, in the face of no small difficulties, has been an unfathomable gift. Thank you for all.

NOTES

PROLOGUE

1. Gabriel Quiroga de San Antonio, *A Brief and Truthful Relation of Events in the Kingdom of Cambodia.* (1604; repr., Bangkok: White Lotus Press, 1998).

2. Alain Fressanges, *Khmer Sayings* (Phnom Penh: Khmer Community Development Publishing, 2009).

3. Klairung Amratisha, "The Cambodian Novel: A Study of Its Emergence and Development" (PhD diss., SOAS University of London, 1998).

4. Jules Marcel Brossard de Corbigny, *Elephant Train: Phnom Penh to Bangkok in 1871*, trans. Jim Mizerski (Phnom Penh: Jasmine Image Machine, 2017).

5. Etienne Fluet-Chouinard, Simon Funge-Smith, and Peter B. McIntyre, "Global Hidden Harvest of Freshwater Fish Revealed by Household Surveys," *Proceedings of the National Academy of Sciences* 115, no. 29 (July 2018): 7623.

6. Fluet-Chouinard, Funge-Smith, and McIntyre, "Global Hidden Harvest," 7623.

7. Food and Agriculture Organization of the United Nations (FAO), *The State of World Fisheries and Aquaculture 2020: Sustainability in Action*, State of World Fisheries and Aquaculture (SOFIA) 2020 (Rome: FAO, 2020), http://www.fao.org/documents/card/en/c/ca9229en.

8. Brian Eyler and Courtney Weatherby, "New Evidence: How China Turned Off the Tap on the Mekong River," Stimson Center, April 13, 2020, https://www.stimson.org/2020/new-evidence-how-china-turned-off-the-mekong-tap/.

9. "Weekly Situation Report for the Wet Season in the Mekong River Basin," Mekong River Commission, August 4, 2020, http://ffw.mrcmekong.org/weekly_report/2020/.

1. THE TIGER DEPENDS ON THE FOREST

1. Alessandro Marazzi Sassoon, "Tonle Sap Forests Razed by Fire," *Phnom Penh Post*, May 26, 2016, https://www.phnompenhpost.com/national/tonle-sap-forests-razed-fire.

2. Zhou Daguan, *A Record of Cambodia: The Land and Its People*, trans. and ed. Peter Harris (Bangkok: Silkworm Books, 2007).

3. "Yields from Fishing Take a Dive," *Phnom Penh Post*, October 28, 2015, https://www.phnompenhpost.com/business/yields-fishing-take-dive.

4. J. T. Fasullo, B. L. Otto-Bliesner, and S. Stevenson, "ENSO's Changing Influence on Temperature, Precipitation, and Wildfire in a Warming Climate," *Geophysical Research Letters* 45, no. 17 (2018): 9216–25.

5. "2020 Closes a Decade of Exceptional Heat," World Meteorological Organization, December 24, 2020, https://public.wmo.int/en/media/news/2020-closes-decade-of-exceptional-heat.

6. David Chandler, *A History of Cambodia*, 2nd ed. (Bangkok: Silkworm Books, 1993).

7. Damian H. Evans, Roland J. Fletcher, Christophe Pottier, Jean-Baptiste Chevance, Dominique Soutif, Boun Suy Tan, Sokrithy Im, Darith Ea, Tina Tin, Samnang Kim, Christopher Cromarty, Stéphane De Greef, Kasper Hanus, Pierre Bâty, Robert Kuszinger, Ichita Shimoda, and Glenn Boornazian, "Uncovering Archaeological Landscapes at Angkor Using Lidar," *Proceedings of the National Academy of Sciences* 110, no. 31 (July 2013): 12595–600.

8. Damian Evans, "Airborne Laser Scanning as a Method for Exploring Long-Term Socio-Ecological Dynamics in Cambodia," *Journal of Archaeological Science* 74 (October 2016): 164–75.

9. Bernard Philippe Groslier, "La cité hydraulique angkorienne: Exploitation ou surexploitation du sol?," *Bulletin de l'École Française d'Extrême-Orient* 66 (1979): 161–202. For an English translation, see Terry Lustig and Christophe Pottier, "The Angkorian Hydraulic City: Exploitation or Over-Exploitation of the Soil? Translation into English of Groslier, B.-P. Le Cité Hydraulique Angkorienne: Exploitation ou Surexploitation du Sol? Bulletin de l'École Française d'Extrême Orient 66, 161–202, 1979," *Aséanie* 20 (December 2007): 133–85.

10. Matti Kummu, "Water Management in Angkor: Human Impacts on Hydrology and Sediment Transportation," *Journal of Environmental Management* 90, no. 3 (March 2009): 1413–21.

11. Chandler, *History of Cambodia*. There remains debate as to whether these reservoirs offered a functional, agricultural purpose or were erected primarily for religious reasons.

12. Brendan M. Buckley, Kevin J. Anchukaitis, Daniel Penny, Roland Fletcher, Edward R. Cook, Masaki Sano, Le Canh Nam, Aroonut Wichienkeeo, Ton That Minh, and Truong Mai Hong, "Climate as a Contributing Factor in the Demise of Angkor, Cambodia," *Proceedings of the National Academy of Sciences* 107, no. 15 (April 2010): 6748–52.

13. Henri Mouhot, *Travels in the Central Parts of Indo-China, Cambodia, and Laos during the Years 1858, 1859, and 1860* (digitized by the Internet Archive in 2010 with funding from Boston Library Consortium, n.d.), accessed July 14, 2021, https://www.gutenberg.org/files/46559/46559-h/46559-h.htm.

2. WHERE THERE IS WATER

1. Henri Mouhot, *Travels in the Central Parts of Indo-China, Cambodia, and Laos during the Years 1858, 1859, and 1860* (digitized by the Internet Archive in 2010 with funding from Boston Library Consortium, n.d.), accessed July 14, 2021, https://www.gutenberg.org/files/46559/46559-h/46559-h.htm.

2. Melissa Marschke, "Governing a Coveted Resource," in Marschke, *Life, Fish and Mangroves: Resource Governance in Coastal Cambodia* (Ottawa: University of Ottawa Press, 2012), 39–56.

3. "Overcoming Factors of Unsustainability and Overexploitation in Fisheries: Selected Papers on Issues and Approaches," Food and Agriculture Organization of the United Nations, accessed February 26, 2021, http://www.fao.org/3/A0312E/A0312E16.htm#ref2.86.

4. "Overcoming Factors of Unsustainability and Overexploitation."

5. Sophanarith Kim, Nophea Kim Phat, Masao Koike, and Hiromichi Hayashi, "Causes of Historical Deforestation and Forest Degradation in Cambodia," *Journal of Forest Planning* 11 (January 2005): 23–31.

6. "Cambodia's Forests Are Disappearing," NASA Earth Observatory, January 10, 2017, https://earthobservatory.nasa.gov/images/89413/cambodias-forests-are-disappearing.

7. Asian Development Bank, *The Tonle Sap Basin Strategy* (Manila: ADB, 2005).

8. Tyson R. Roberts, "Fish Scenes, Symbolism, and Kingship in the Bas-Reliefs of Angkor Wat and the Bayon," *Natural History Bulletin of the Siam Society* 50, no. 2 (2002): 135–93.

9. Vandy Rattana's moving photo and video series *Bomb Ponds* explores these omnipresent craters. See more at https://www.guggenheim.org/video/vandy-rattanas-bomb-ponds-photographs-and-video (accessed July 25, 2021).

10. *Krom samaki*, or solidarity groups, were a fairly liberal form of collectivization imposed on fishing and farming communities during the Vietnamese occupation of the 1980s. They varied greatly in scope and size, with the

groups either dividing the catch and crop among themselves, or selling it off. In the late 1980s, as Cambodia began transitioning to self-rule, *krom samaki* were abandoned in favor of open markets. For the fisheries, that meant a return to the revenue-generating lots system. Meanwhile, on land, the rapid dissolution contributed to the land titling chaos that plagues Cambodia to this day. For more information, see Kyoko Kusakabe, Wang Yunxian, and Govind Kelkar, "Women and Land Rights in Cambodia." *Economic and Political Weekly* 30, no. 43 (October 1995): WS87–S92. Also see Marschke, "Governing a Coveted Resource."

11. Vuthy Voeun, "Late Prehistoric Site in Cambodia Yields Thousands of Fish Bones from 18 Families," *Catch and Culture* 16, no. 2 (August 2010): 13–18.

3. DON'T LET A HUNGRY MAN GUARD RICE

1. Jules Marcel Brossard de Corbigny, *Elephant Train: Phnom Penh to Bangkok in 1871*, trans. Jim Mizerski (Phnom Penh: Jasmine Image Machine, 2017).

2. "List of Freshwater Fishes Reported from Cambodia," FishBase, accessed February 28, 2021, https://www.fishbase.se/country/CountryChecklist.php ?showAll=yes&what=list&trpp=50&c_code=116&sortby=alpha2&ext_CL= on&ext_pic=on&vhabitat=fresh.

3. *General Population Census of the Kingdom of Cambodia: National Report on Final Census Results*, National Institute of Statistics, Cambodian Ministry of Planning, October 2020, https://www.nis.gov.kh/nis/Census2019/Final %20General%20Population%20Census%202019-English.pdf.

4. Thol Dina and Jin Sato, "The Cost of Dividing the Commons: Overlapping Property Systems in Tonle Sap, Cambodia," *International Journal of the Commons* 9 (March 2015): 261–80.

5. P. Degen and N. Thouk, "Inland Fishery Management in Cambodia: Is the Fishing Lot System the Basis for Improved Management or Should It Be Abolished?" (paper presented at the 7th Biennial Conference of the International Association for the Study of Common Property, Vancouver, June 10–14, 1998).

6. Chea Sotheacheath and Matthew Grainger, "The Great Lake: Fish, Guns, Money and Fences," *Phnom Penh Post*, December 11, 1998, https://www .phnompenhpost.com/national/great-lake-fish-guns-money-and-fences.

7. Vong Sokheng and May Kunmakara, "Hun Sen Bans Industry Fishing at Tonle Sap Lake Permanently," *Phnom Penh Post*, February 29, 2012, https:// www.phnompenhpost.com/business/hun-sen-bans-industry-fishing-tonle -sap-lake-permanently.

8. Sotheary Pech, "Crackdown on Fisheries Crimes," *Khmer Times*, February 5, 2019, https://www.khmertimeskh.com/575552/crackdown-on-fisheries-crimes/.

9. Kate Bandler, "Illegal Fishing around the Tonle Sap," Focus on the Global South, 2017, https://focusweb.org/wp-content/uploads/2018/12/Cambodia-Illegal-Fishing-Report-A4.pdf.

10. Van Roeun, "Illegal Fishing Task Force for Tonle Sap Lake Claims Success," *Cambodia Daily*, April 19, 2017, https://english.cambodiadaily.com/news/illegal-fishing-task-force-for-tonle-sap-lake-claims-success-128213/.

4. NAVIGATE A RIVER

1. E. Baran et al., "Fish Resources in Cambodia (2001–2011)," in *Atlas of Cambodia: Maps on Socio-Economic Development and Environment*, ed. Rebeca Sandoval (Phnom Penh: Save Cambodia's Wildlife, 2014), 37–48.

2. Ian Baird, Mark Flaherty, and Bounpheng Phylavanh, "Rhythms of the River: Lunar Phases and Migrations of Small Carps (Cyprinidae) in the Mekong River," *Natural History Bulletin of the Siam Society* 51, no. 1 (January 2003): 5–36.

3. Mekong River Commission, *Overview of the Hydrology of the Mekong River Basin* (Vientiane, Laos: Mekong River Commission, 2005), http://www.mekonginfo.org/assets/midocs/0001968-inland-waters-overview-of-the-hydrology-of-the-mekong-basin.pdf.

4. Brian Eyler and Courtney Weatherby, "Mekong Mainstream Dams," Stimson Center, June 23, 2020, https://www.stimson.org/2020/mekong-mainstream-dams/.

5. Brian Eyler and Courtney Weatherby, "New Evidence: How China Turned Off the Tap on the Mekong River," Stimson Center, April 13, 2020, https://www.stimson.org/2020/new-evidence-how-china-turned-off-the-mekong-tap/.

6. Eyler and Weatherby, "New Evidence."

7. Eyler and Weatherby, "Mekong Mainstream Dams."

8. Sovannarith Keo, "Drought, Dams on Mekong River Drop Cambodia's Tonle Sap Lake to Record Low Levels," Radio Free Asia, July 27, 2020, https://www.rfa.org/english/news/cambodia/lake-07272020174242.html.

9. Jeffrey W. Jacobs, "Mekong Committee History and Lessons for River Basin Development," *Geographical Journal* 161, no. 2 (July 1995): 135–48.

10. Victor J. Croizat, "The Mekong River Development Project: Some Geographical, Historical, and Political Considerations" (report for the Rand

Corporation, January 1, 1967), https://www.rand.org/pubs/papers
/P3616.html.

11. Jacobs, "Mekong Committee History."

12. Eyler and Weatherby, "Mekong Mainstream Dams."

13. Guy Ziv, Eric Baran, So Nam, Ignacio Rodríguez-Iturbe, and Simon A.
Levin, "Trading-off Fish Biodiversity, Food Security, and Hydropower in the
Mekong River Basin," *Proceedings of the National Academy of Sciences* 109,
no. 15 (April 2012): 5609–14.

14. Prach Chev, "Cambodian Villagers Threaten Renewed Protests against Dam
Developer—Radio Free Asia," Radio Free Asia, March 2, 2015, https://www
.rfa.org/english/news/cambodia/dam-03022015173133.html.

15. Ministry of Mines and Energy of Cambodia, "Cambodia Basic Energy
Plan," Economic Research Institute for ASEAN and East Asia, 2019, http://
www.eria.org/publications/cambodia-basic-energy-plan/.

16. Dene-Hern Chen and Naren Kuch, "Electricity Vietnam No Longer
Involved in Lower Sesan 2 Dam," *Cambodia Daily*, November 28, 2012,
https://english.cambodiadaily.com/news/electricity-vietnam-no-longer
-involved-in-lower-sesan-2-dam-6363/.

17. "Sesan Dam Law Approved," *Radio Free Asia*, February 15, 2013, https://
www.rfa.org/english/news/sesan-02152013182113.htm.

18. Abby Seiff, "In the Mekong, Questions Arise over Impact of Favoring
Hydropower," Devex, April 11, 2018, https://www.devex.com/news/in-the
-mekong-questions-arise-over-impact-of-favoring-hydropower-92384.

19. Mekong River Commission, "Key Messages of the Council Study Reports,"
March 2018, https://www.mrcmekong.org/assets/Publications/Council
-Study/Key-messages-of-the-Council-Study-reports_26-Nov-18_revised-4
-Jan-19.pdf.

20. Mekong River Commission, "Key Messages."

21. Joerg Hartmann, "Reconsidering the Sambor and Stung Treng Hydropower
Projects: Synthesis Brief," World Wildlife Federation, 2018, https://wwfasia
.awsassets.panda.org/downloads/sambor___stung_treng_brief_wwf.pdf.

5. THE ANT EATS THE FISH

1. Mekong River Commission, "Mekong Basin-Wide Fisheries Management
and Development Strategy 2018–2022," November 2017, https://www
.mrcmekong.org/assets/Publications/BFMS-Feb20-v-Final.pdf.

2. O. Lang, "Current Status of Sustainable Aquaculture in Cambodia," in
*Resource Enhancement and Sustainable Aquaculture Practices in Southeast
Asia: Challenges in Responsible Production of Aquatic Species: Proceedings of the*

International Workshop on Resource Enhancement and Sustainable Aquaculture Practices in Southeast Asia 2014, ed. Maria Rowena R. Romana-Eguia, Fe D. Parado-Estepa, Nerissa D. Salayo, and Ma. Junemie Hazel Lebata-Ramos (Tigbauan, Iloilo, Philippines: Aquaculture Department of the Southeast Asian Fisheries Development Center), 27–40.

3. Sophanith Phal, "Aquaculture Sector Takes Off in Cambodia," *Khmer Times*, July 9, 2020, https://www.khmertimeskh.com/50743003/aquaculture-sector -takes-off-in-cambodia/.

4. So Nam, Sam Narith, Bui Minh Tam, Tran Thi Thanh Hien, and Robert S. Pomeroy, "Sustainable Snakehead Aquaculture Development in the Lower Mekong River Basin of Cambodia and Vietnam Indigenous Species Development; Part 1: Breeding and Weaning of Striped Snakehead (*Channa Striata*) in Cambodia," in *Technical Reports 2009–2011*, vol. 1, AquaFish Collaborative Research Support Program (Corvallis: Oregon State University, 2012), 289–301, https://aquafishcrsp.oregonstate.edu/sites/aquafishcrsp .oregonstate.edu/files/09firvo l_1_aug2012.pdf.

5. Le Sinh, Hap Navy, and Robert Pomeroy, "Value Chain of Snakehead Fish in the Lower Mekong Basin of Cambodia and Vietnam," *Aquaculture Economics and Management* 18 (January 2014): 76–96.

6. Aun Pheap, "Ministry Wants Snakehead Fish Farms Again," *Cambodia Daily*, April 22, 2016, https://english.cambodiadaily.com/news/ministry -wants-snakehead-fish-farms-again-111619/.

7. Sar Kapun, "Danle Sap Yoeng," in *The Heart of the Poet*, trans. Neou Vannarin (Phnom Penh: Cultural Publishing Institute, 1985), 14–16.

8. Sarath Sorn, "PM Wants to Use COVID Crisis to Reform Agriculture," *Khmer Times*, July 15, 2020, https://www.khmertimeskh.com/50745293/pm-wants -to-use-covid-crisis-to-reform-agriculture/.

9. Hin Pisei, "Fisheries Output near 1M Tonnes," *Phnom Penh Post*, December 23, 2020, https://www.phnompenhpost.com/business/fisheries-output-near -1m-tonnes.

10. "$17M Aqua-Feed Program in Cambodia Launch—Growing America," Kansas State University, February 7, 2019, https://www.growingamerica.com /news/2019/02/17m-aqua-feed-program-cambodia-launch.

11. "Fish Farm Project on the Table," *Phnom Penh Post*, January 20, 2017, https://www.phnompenhpost.com/business/fish-farm-project-table.

6. THE GOD OF MERCY

1. George Groslier, *Water and Light: A Travel Journal of the Cambodian Mekong*, ed. Kent Davis (Holmes Beach FL: DatAsia Press, 2016).

2. "Population Size," *General Population Census of the Kingdom of Cambodia: National Report on Final Census Results*, National Institute of Statistics, Ministry of Planning, October 2020, p. 13, https://www.nis.gov.kh/nis/Census2019 /Final%20General%20Population%20Census%202019-English.pdf.

3. Michael Cooperman et al., "A Watershed Moment for the Mekong: Newly Announced Community Use and Conservation Areas for the Tonle Sap Lake May Boost Sustainability of the World's Largest Inland Fishery," *Cambodian Journal of Natural History* 2012 (December 1, 2012): 101–6.

7. ONE HUNDRED DAYS OF TEARS

1. "Ethnic Vietnamese," Minority Rights Group, 2017, https://minorityrights .org/minorities/ethnic-vietnamese/.

2. Jules Marcel Brossard de Corbigny, *Elephant Train: Phnom Penh to Bangkok in 1871*, trans. Jim Mizerski (Phnom Penh: Jasmine Image Machine, 2017).

3. Henri Mouhot, *Travels in the Central Parts of Indo-China, Cambodia, and Laos during the Years 1858, 1859, and 1860* (digitized by the Internet Archive in 2010 with funding from Boston Library Consortium, n.d.), accessed July 14, 2021, https://www.gutenberg.org/files/46559/46559-h/46559-h.htm.

4. Louis de Carné, *Travels on the Mekong: Cambodia, Laos and Yunnan: The Political and Trade Report of the Mekong Exploration Commission, June 1866– June 1868* (Bangkok: White Lotus Press, 1995).

5. For more on charities, see Sophal Ear, *Aid Dependence in Cambodia: How Foreign Assistance Undermines Democracy* (New York: Columbia University Press, 2012).

8. FROGS GET LOST IN LAKES

1. Vireak Thou, "Migrant Remittances Total $2.8B Last Year," *Phnom Penh Post*, February 23, 2020, https://www.phnompenhpost.com/business /migrant-remittances-total-28b-last-year.

2. "Collateral Damage: Land Loss and Abuses in Cambodia's Microfinance Sector," Cambodian League for the Promotion and Defense of Human Rights (Licadho), August 7, 2019, https://www.licadho-cambodia.org /reports.php?perm=228.

3. Robert Carmichael, "Interest Cap Poses Body Blow for Cambodian Microfinance," Voice of America, March 27, 2017, https://www.voanews.com/east -asia-pacific/interest-cap-poses-body-blow-cambodian-microfinance; "Cambodia: Micro-Loan Borrowers Face Covid-19 Crisis," Human Rights Watch, July 14, 2020, https://www.hrw.org/news/2020/07/14/cambodia-micro-loan -borrowers-face-covid-19-crisis.

4. George Steptoe, "Cambodian Flood Victims Drowning in Debt," *Diplomat*, October 22, 2013, https://thediplomat.com/2013/10/cambodian-flood -victims-drowning-in-debt/.

5. Zhou Daguan, *A Record of Cambodia: The Land and Its People*, trans. and ed. Peter Harris (Bangkok: Silkworm Books, 2007).

6. Peter Degen and Nao Thuok, "Inland Fishery Management in Cambodia: Is the Fishing Lot System the Basis for Improved Management or Should It Be Abolished?," Project for Management of the Freshwater Capture Fisheries of Cambodia, Mekong River Commission, 1998, https://dlc.dlib.indiana.edu /dlc/bitstream/handle/10535/1635/degen.pdf?sequence=1&isAllowed=y.

7. Margaret Slocomb, *An Economic History of Cambodia in the Twentieth Century* (Singapore: NUS Press, 2010).

8. Adolf Bastian, *Journey in Cambodia and Cochin-China (1864)* (Bangkok: White Lotus Press, 2005).

9. Henri Mouhot, *Travels in the Central Parts of Indo-China, Cambodia, and Laos during the Years 1858, 1859, and 1860* (digitized by the Internet Archive in 2010 with funding from Boston Library Consortium, n.d.), accessed July 14, 2021, https://www.gutenberg.org/files/46559/46559-h/46559-h.htm.

10. Mouhot, *Travels in the Central Parts of Indo-China, Cambodia, and Laos.*

9. BROKEN GLASS FLOATS

1. Louis de Carné, *Travels on the Mekong: Cambodia, Laos and Yunnan: The Political and Trade Report of the Mekong Exploration Commission, June 1866– June 1868* (Bangkok: White Lotus Press, 1995).

2. Adolf Bastian, *Journey in Cambodia and Cochin-China (1864)* (Bangkok: White Lotus Press, 2005).

3. The same 2004 drought that allowed Voeurn Vuthy to unearth burial mounds near the Tonle Sap was used to dispel the road myth. Core samples taken from the Tonle Sap permitted diligent, if a bit killjoy, researchers to put an end to the theorizing once and for all. Read more at: C. Pottier, D. Penny, M. Hendrickson, and E. A. Carter, "Unearthing an Atlantean Myth in Angkor: Geoarchaeological Investigation of the 'Underwater Road' Crossing the Tonle Sap Lake, Cambodia," *Journal of Archaeological Science* 39, no. 8 (August 2012): 2604–11.

4. This paragraph pulls descriptions from the following texts: Jules Marcel Brossard de Corbigny, *Elephant Train: Phnom Penh to Bangkok in 1871*, trans. Jim Mizerski (Phnom Penh: Jasmine Image Machine, 2017); Zhou Daguan, *A Record of Cambodia: The Land and Its People*, trans. and ed. Peter Harris (Bangkok: Silkworm Books, 2007); Gabriel Quiroga de San Antonio, *A*

Brief and Truthful Relation of Events in the Kingdom of Cambodia. (1604; repr., Bangkok: White Lotus Press, 1998); Henri Mouhot, *Travels in the Central Parts of Indo-China, Cambodia, and Laos during the Years 1858, 1859, and 1860* (digitized by the Internet Archive in 2010 with funding from Boston Library Consortium, n.d.), accessed August 17, 2021, https://www.gutenberg .org/files/46559/46559-h/46559-h.htm; and Bastian, *Journey in Cambodia.*

5. De Carné, *Travels on the Mekong.*

6. "Flash Floods from Collapsed Lao Dam Hit 17 Villages in NE Cambodia," *Xinhua*, July 25, 2018, http://www.xinhuanet.com/english/2018-07/25/c _137348022.htm.

7. Mekong River Commission, "Mekong Water Levels Reach Low Record," July 18, 2019, https://www.mrcmekong.org/news-and-events/news/mekong -water-levels-reach-low-record/.

8. Prapan Chankaew, "Drought Reveals Lost Temple in Thailand Submerged by Dam," Reuters, August 5, 2019, https://www.reuters.com/article /us-thailand-drought-temple/drought-reveals-lost-temple-in-thailand -submerged-by-dam-idUSKCN1UW023.

9. "Severe Drought in Mekong Region Reduces Rice Planting in Laos," Radio Free Asia, July 26, 2019, https://www.rfa.org/english/news/laos/severe -drought-in-mekong-region-07262019164116.html.

10. Zoe Osborne, "The Great Salt Drought Desiccating Vietnam's Mekong Delta," Al Jazeera, April 22, 2020, https://www.aljazeera.com/features/2020 /4/22/the-great-salt-drought-desiccating-vietnams-mekong-delta.

11. Mekong River Commission, "Weekly Situation Report for the Wet Season in the Mekong River Basin," September 28, 2020, http://ffw.mrcmekong.org /weekly_report/2020/Weekly%20flood%20&%20drought%20situation %20report%2022-28%20Sept_Final.pdf.

12. Brian Eyler, "Tonle Sap Bottleneck Comparison—September 2019 vs 2020," September 18, 2020, https://www.planet.com/stories/tonle-sap-bottleneck -comparison-september-2019-vs--uyecQ-dGg.

13. Mekong River Commission, "Weekly Situation Report," September 28, 2020.

14. Interviews conducted by Mech Dara.

15. Thomas Cristofoletti, "The Last Breath of the Tonle Sap," *South China Morning Post*, January 7, 2021, YouTube video, 10:27, https://www.youtube .com/watch?v=14zCeR2GEF8.

INDEX

Italicized figure numbers refer to photographs following page 60.

CPSIA information can be obtained
at www.ICGtesting.com
Printed in the USA
LVHW011121090322
712947LV00006B/122